Teach Your Kids to Swim

Tips and tricks for fun-for-everyone swimming lessons

KAREN MURPHY

Copyright © 2017 Karen Murphy

All rights reserved.

No liability is assumed for damages resulting from the use of information in this book.

ISBN: 1544666268

ISBN-13: 978-1544666266

DEDICATION

To my wonderful son and husband, who put up with all of the writing and splashing around.

Contents

Preface 1
Introduction 3
    How to use this book 4
    A note about language 5
    Ready, set, splash! 5
Chapter 1 Getting Your Head in the Right Place 7
    Understand what to expect from your child 7
        What water safety means 8
        What water safety doesn't mean 8
        How long it will take 9
    Understand what to expect from yourself 9
        Patience 10
        Positive attitude 10
        What you bring to the water 10
        Respect for your child's feelings 11
        Respect for your child's developmental stage 12
    Take steps to stay focused 12
Chapter 2 What It Feels Like for a Kid 15
    Kids' bodies 15
        Head size 16
        Limb length 16
        Lung capacity 16
        BMI 17
        Buoyancy 17
        Rest 17
    Kids' sensory experience 17
        Touch, sight, and hearing 17
        Proprioception 18
        Breathing 18
        Body heat 18
        The role of rest 19
        How to meet your child's needs 19
    Kids' feelings 20
        Fear 20
        How to address fear 21

  Anger 21
  How to address anger...22
  Happiness..22
  Security 22
  Pride 23
 Kids' motivation 23
 Kids' perceptions of success 24
 Kids' abilities 25
  Kids' abilities by age 26
Chapter 3 Getting a Head Start...29
 How kids learn 29
  Kids learn by playing 30
  Kids learn by figuring it out themselves 30
  Kids learn in short spurts..31
  Kids need lots of practice 31
  Kids sometimes get stuck 31
 How kids learn physical skills 32
 Feelings matter 33
 Swimming 33
  Finesse 33
  Rhythm 34
  Power 34
  Drag 34
  Relaxation..35
  Ease..35
 The big picture 35
Chapter 4 Safety First..37
 The environment 37
  Weather 37
  Pools 38
  Open water 40
 Behavior...40
  Preparation..41
  Kids..41
  Grownups, too 43
 In case of emergency...44
Chapter 5 Before You Start 45
 Preparation for getting into the pool...45

- Toys and equipment 45
- What to wear 46
- Things to do 47
- Preparation for getting out of the pool 48
- Chapter 6 Your First Time at the Pool 51
  - When you get there 51
  - Getting in 52
  - The most important thing 53
- Chapter 7 How to Teach 55
  - The fundamentals 56
  - Creating the atmosphere 56
  - Crafting a teaching style 57
    - Explaining 57
    - Demonstrating and setting an example 59
    - Exploring 59
    - Observing 61
    - Giving praise and support 62
    - Giving feedback and corrections 62
    - Giving physical feedback 64
    - Going with the flow 65
  - Structuring lessons 66
    - Lesson outline 66
    - Lay the groundwork 67
    - Getting into the pool 67
    - Reviewing what you've already learned 68
    - Playing 69
    - Teaching something new 69
    - Practicing the new skill 70
    - Playing (again!) 71
  - Being attuned to your child 72
  - Making the most of your time in the water 74
  - Bringing the lessons out of the pool 74
    - Observe 75
    - Move 75
    - Relax 76
    - Visualize 77
  - Putting it all together 77
- Chapter 8 What to Do: 49 Tricks to Make Lessons Fun and Effective 79

  Do create an atmosphere that's conducive to learning 79
  Do make the most of time in the water 80
  Do fine-tune your teaching style 80
  Do be attuned to your child's needs 82
Chapter 9 What Not to Do: Fifteen Sure-fire Ways to Keep Your Lesson Afloat 83
  Don't lose your child's trust 83
  Don't send your child subtle messages that they should fear the water 84
  Don't let your expectations interfere with your child's progress 84
Chapter 10 What Your Child Needs to Learn 85
  Sequence of skills 86
    Getting into the pool 87
    Feeling the water 91
    Holding onto the wall and climbing out 93
    Blowing bubbles 94
    Putting their head underwater 97
    Kicking 99
    Gliding in streamline or torpedo position 102
    Popup breathing 104
    Body shape and position 106
    Treading water 108
    Moving underwater 110
    Back float 111
    Front crawl 113
    Backstroke 118
    Turning their head to breathe 121
  Internalizing the skills 125
Chapter 11 Life: A Game, a Play, a Bowl of Cherries 127
  Getting into the pool 128
  Feeling the water 130
  Holding onto the wall and climbing out 131
  Blowing bubbles 132
  Putting their head underwater 133
  Kicking 135
  Gliding in streamline or torpedo position 136
  Popup breathing 137
  Body shape and position 137

Treading water 138
Moving underwater 140
Back float 141
Front crawl 142
Backstroke 143
Turning their head to breathe 144

Preface

Shivering and tears. Even though he was wearing a shorty wetsuit, even though his swimming teacher was friendly and engaging, my sweet little boy was shivering, and he was in tears. Once a week, I sat in the viewing area, biting my lip as I watched him having, at best, no fun at all. There had to be a better way for him to learn to swim, and I decided to figure out what it was.

I pulled from my background as a researcher, a preschool teacher assistant, and an occasional lifeguard. I studied child development and psychology and the mechanics of swimming. I interviewed swimming teachers and other lifeguards.

I was confident that I'd figured out a system that would be fun and effective. To make sure, I threw on a swimsuit and practiced the techniques with my son, and then with my friends and their kids, and then with their friends and their kids, refining as we went.

And you know what? It worked! Understanding the obstacles and challenges specific to kids was critical to understanding how to make learning to swim fun for them, and adding the presence of a trusted and loved parent turned the experience of learning to swim into something the kids—and their parents—treasured.

Today I asked my son, now almost a teenager and half fish, what his favorite part of having learned to swim from me was. He said it was the adventure and the family bonding. For me, I felt great that I was giving him critical safety skills as well as swimming ability that would bring him pleasure for the rest of his life. More than that, though, what I loved was knowing that his experience, and mine, was transformed into something fun and joyful. That's what I wish for you and your family.

Happy splashing!

Introduction

This book is all about helping you keep your kids safe and happy by providing you with the information and steps to teach swimming and water safety. Beyond that, you'll learn to do it in a way that's fun and intuitive for you and your kids.

What is this information? What are these steps?

First, you'll need to understand some basic concepts. Next you'll need to understand how to teach swimming. Finally, you'll need to know the skills to teach and specifically how to teach each skill.

Chapters 1 through 6 will give you the underlying concepts that you'll need to teach your kids to swim safely and happily.

- You'll learn to understand what to expect from your child when it comes to swimming lessons, and you'll learn to establish reasonable expectations for yourself. I'll show you how to take steps to keep the mindset that will make teaching your child to swim fun. That will pave the way for a joyful, productive learning experience for both of you.

- To set you up for success, you'll learn to understand how your child's body, feelings, and perceptions come into play when they're learning to swim and how they differ from those of adults.

- You'll learn how to maintain a safe swimming environment and how to teach your child behavior that promotes safety.

- You'll learn which supplies you'll need, how to prepare your child, and how to prepare your plan before you go to the pool, as well as what you'll need to have waiting when you get out of the pool.

- You'll learn how to approach your first time at the pool with a mindset and plan designed to establish the tone for all of the lessons you and your child will share.

- You'll learn some key concepts about how kids learn, special aspects of their physical learning, the role of feelings in learning, and key characteristics of swimming.

Chapters 7 through 9 will give you detailed instructions for developing your insights and creative reservoirs and learning how to structure swimming lessons, optimize how they work, and adapt them to your child's needs on the fly. You'll get detailed tips for how to be effective as a teacher.

Chapter 10, the longest chapter in the book, will teach you the meaning of water safety and the detailed steps to teach your child the skills they needs to be water safe.

Chapter 11 details more than 150 games and activities tailored to making each skill fun to learn and teach.

How to use this book

I recommend that you start by reading the whole book but skimming Chapter 10. Reread the chapter on teaching after your first lesson or anytime you need to remind yourself of the details. As you plan each lesson, reread the sections in Chapter 10 and in the appendix addressing the skill you'll be teaching.

A note about language

I wish English had a gender-neutral singular pronoun. Because it doesn't, I'll use the words "they" and "them" and "their" even when I'm talking about just one person. What can you do? That's English for you: always forcing you to make the tough choices.

Ready, set, splash!

You're doing your child a great service by teaching them to swim. You're helping to keep them safe, and providing them with a skill they'll enjoy for the rest of their life, either on its own or as a necessary part of the vast array of great water sports. What are you waiting for? Dive in!

Chapter 1
Getting Your Head in the Right Place

Teaching your child to swim can be a celebration of your relationship, punctuated by fun, hugs and laughter. It can also be a miserable experience for both of you. It all depends on your expectations and on your approach. Before you even think about getting into the pool, you need to decide how to make sure your expectations and approach are designed to make sure the experience is a joyful and productive one.

Understand what to expect from your child

Your goal is to teach your child to be safe in the water.

What water safety means

Being water safe means your child has the skills they need to maneuver in the water with control and confidence. Good indicators that your child has gotten to this point are:

- They can swim the width or length of the pool, easily taking breaths as necessary.

- They can tread water for at least three minutes in any depth.

- They can get into the pool by themselves easily, either by jumping in from the side or from a seated position on the edge of the pool.

- They can get out of the pool by themselves easily, by grabbing the side of the pool and pulling themselves out or by swimming to the stairs or ladder and climbing out.

- They can pick things up from the bottom of the pool.

What water safety doesn't mean

- It doesn't mean that you've removed all risk. Swimming, like the rest of life, will never be completely without risk.

- It doesn't mean being able to swim without adult supervision. No one, including an adult, should ever swim alone.

- It doesn't mean being a competitive swimmer. Mastering the major strokes requires many hours of committed training. It also requires a high level of motor development. Your child's level of coordination in the water will look a lot like their coordination on land.

How long it will take

How long it takes is completely dependent on you and your child.

- Where is your child physically, mentally and emotionally?

- How creative are you?

- How comfortable is your child with the water already?

- How motivated is your child? (Having older siblings or friends who get to play and have fun in the water because they know how to swim motivates most kids.)

- How sensitive is your child to physical stimuli?

- Does your child like novelty or the familiar?

A big shift in skill and ability will happen when your child learns to relax in the water. Ironically, it's hard to relax in the water until you have enough skill to feel comfortable. One of the most important things you'll work on is getting comfortable in the water without putting any pressure on achieving that goal.

Understand what to expect from yourself

Your goal is to make it fun, for yourself and your child.

Don't expect yourself to be perfect at this, and don't expect teaching your child to swim to be easy all the time. If you keep your goal in mind, though, you can maintain the perspective you need to make teaching your child to swim an experience you'll both enjoy.

Patience

If you go into this process with a deadline in mind, you're setting yourself up for disappointment. Be patient with your child and with yourself. Don't rush things. Think of the process as being as important as the goal.

Your patience will let your child relax and explore, which are both critical to learning. Your patience will also let *you* relax and explore. You'll have the ability to pay full attention to your child's progress without judging it, so you'll be a better teacher. You won't put pressure on your child or yourself, so you'll both be able to enjoy each other and the process.

When you're patient, you increase the possibility of finding joy in each lesson. Your child will associate that joy with the lessons and with swimming.

Of course, no parent is perfect at being patient all the time. (Ah, if only it were so easy.) But keeping patience in mind as one of your major goals—a more powerful goal than any other outcome during a given lesson—might help you stay focused on the process.

Positive attitude

While you may be focused on what you're trying to accomplish, don't forget to give your child plenty of encouragement, both in and out of the water. Be sincere and positive. Remind them that what you're doing together is going to keep them safe and healthy and that it's going to be lots of fun, especially in the long term.

What you bring to the water

Ideally, you should have basic water safety, CPR, and first aid training. The Red Cross and hospitals often offer this training.

Kids read your body language and are attuned to your mental and emotional state. They're aware of tension in your body and whether your breathing is slow and steady or fast and shallow.

If you're afraid or concerned, your child will pick up on that. Until you're over your own fear, you're not in a good position to teach your child. (Rather, you're in the perfect position to pass your fear on to them.) In fact, if you're afraid, it's going to be tougher for your child even if you're not the one doing the teaching.

Prepare yourself before you go into the water by focusing on and visualizing your plan for your time in the water with your child. Remind yourself to let go of concerns about other things. Remind yourself that you're doing something wonderful for your child's health, safety, and future. Remind yourself that you want this lesson to be fun for both of you. Smile and take some deep breaths.

Before you get into the pool, give your child a hug, a kiss, and a smile, and tell them you love them. You'll set the tone for the lesson, and it will be serene, gently focused, loving, and effective.

Respect for your child's feelings

Don't deny or minimize what your child is feeling. Acknowledge it, be direct about it, and be matter-of-fact about it. Whether your child is angry about having to be uncomfortable or try something new, afraid of the water, happy about the opportunity to play with you, or proud of the progress they're making, they'll feel secure when you acknowledge their feelings.

There's no need to be dramatic about it. Remain calm. All you have to do is say, "So you're feeling angry? I can understand that. You're feeling afraid? I can understand that." Acknowledging and respecting the feeling is the first step to moving past the feeling.

If your child is afraid, avoid the knee-jerk reaction to deny their fear. It's not helpful to tell them that there's nothing to be afraid of or that they shouldn't worry. Acknowledge that it's reasonable for them to be afraid.

Until they have the skills to be safe, the water is dangerous. That's a rational fear.

If an activity brings up fear for your child, back off. Inch into it a little at a time. As soon as their fear starts to rise, backtrack to an activity your child is comfortable with and spend plenty of time in that comfortable, confident place.

Respect for your child's developmental stage

Don't compare your child to other kids. Everybody learns at different rates and in different ways. Some things may be easier than others for your child to learn. You may be great at predicting this, but you may also be taken by surprise. Be flexible and be prepared to deal with the reality of your child's experience instead of your expectations of how things should be.

Take steps to stay focused

Keep your eyes on the prize: water safety, making your relationship stronger (not more frustrating or angst-ridden), and teaching your child to associate the water and your lessons with fun and pleasure.

Write the key things you want to focus on and remember on an index card. Read the index card before every lesson.

Ask your child to help you stay focused. Tell them that you plan to be patient and that you want them to be patient, too. Think of a code the two of you can use if the other forgets. How about "apple sauce" as the code for patience? Ask them to use the code if they think you're forgetting to focus on being patient.

You can use different code words for different aspects of attitude or different parts of the goal you want to stay focused on. If you're starting to feel frustrated, hearing your child break out the "apple sauce" code will be enough to bring back your smile and remind you of your priorities. Safe. Fun. Happy.

Chapter 2
What It Feels Like for a Kid

The better you understand what your child is experiencing, the easier and more effective your teaching will be. Children's bodies are different from adults' bodies. So are their feelings and perceptions about swimming and success and their abilities. Understanding these differences will help you to put yourself in your child's place and respond to their needs. Responding to your child's needs will help to make the learning process fun and effective for both of you.

Kids' bodies

It's hard to imagine that someday the kid who hasn't even put their face underwater in the bathtub could be stepping onto the podium to accept an Olympic gold. Safety and fun are the most likely reasons for teaching your child to swim, but just for kicks, let's look at what goes into being a world-class swimmer.

I'm not talking about the obvious thousands of hours of practice and high-tech equipment that athletes turn into seconds shaved from their personal records, and I'm not talking about the minute details like how great swimmers sweat and spread their fingers.

I'm talking about the basics: the swimmer's body.

What does the world-class swimmer's body look like? Tall and lean with long arms and a long torso, big hands, and big feet. Does that sound like your child's body? Probably not.

Head size

If they're anything like the average, your child's head is large compared to the rest of their body. In our early years, our limbs grow more slowly than the head and the rest of the body.

Limb length

Try this cute trick. Ask a toddler how big they are. When they lift their hands, they'll only reach the top of their head. It's adorable, but it makes it tougher for little kids to propel their head-heavy body through the water than it is for an adult, even one who isn't a world-class swimmer. Ask your child to lift their arms straight up. The farther they extend beyond the top of their head, the closer to an adult's their body proportions—and their buoyancy and maneuverability in the water—are likely to be.

Lung capacity

Kids also have less lung capacity than adults do, not only overall but also relative to body mass. The ratio of total lung capacity to BMI in an average seven-year-old boy might be 1:10. In a seventeen-year-old, 1:2.5 is typical. Not only do kids need to take more breaths than adults do, they also aren't as buoyant as adults are.

BMI

Kids' body mass isn't like an adult's. They have a much larger surface area to mass ratio, which means they lose body heat more quickly. Often their body fat percentage is much lower than an adult's, and this also makes them less buoyant.

Buoyancy

Their lower lung capacity and body fat percentage make floating much tougher for kids than it is for adults. They just aren't as buoyant.

Rest

Those growing bodies also mean that kids need more rest than adults do. They go hard and crash hard. Rest and recovery time are important.

Kids' sensory experience

Imagine your child's experience of the water. It's different from their experience on the land in almost every way.

Touch, sight, and hearing

The feel of the water on their body is much heavier than the air they're used to. The extra pressure on their body can feel confining.

Things look weird underwater, and the water feels strange on your eyes. Goggles help if your child is uncomfortable with these sensations.

Your child can't hear well underwater. Sound is muted. The feeling of water getting into their ears and draining out is strange.

Proprioception

Proprioception, your awareness of where your body and its parts are and how they move, changes dramatically in the water for everyone, and it's an unfamiliar sensation for kids.

The way their body balances in the water is different than it is on the land. It will make them feel less coordinated than they do on land.

Their body position is different in the water. On land, we're used to aiming for an upright orientation. In water, horizontal is ideal. You can practice the idea of horizontal on land by having your child crawl or roll on the ground, just to remind them that they've experienced this position and what it feels like, but it will still be an unfamiliar feeling in the water.

Moving through the water feels different. The water resists more than air, so it's harder to move through it. On land, our legs do most of the work moving our bodies around. In the water, our arms and torsos do most of the work.

Breathing

Breathing in the water is different. On land, your child doesn't have to pay attention to the position of their head or the timing of their breathing. They just breathe whenever they need to. In the water, they have to be aware of timing and position or risk getting a big gulp or snort of water.

Body heat

Their body will lose heat faster—up to 25 times faster—in the water than it does on land. Even if they're wearing a wet suit, they'll be starting to cool off from the moment they get into the water.

The role of rest

Rest and recovery time are important not only physically but also for your child's sensory and mental processing of their experience in the water. After they get out of the water, their brain will still be analyzing and creating a cohesive understanding of their time swimming.

How to meet your child's needs

Here are three critical ways to use your awareness of your child's body and sensory experience to fulfill their physical needs.

- **Be on the lookout for physical discomfort.** Physical discomfort can crop up quickly. Remember that your child's body composition makes them more susceptible to cold. They'll be less likely to pace themselves and may suddenly be very tired. Watch for signs that they're hungry, thirsty, or have an upset stomach from swallowing water or air. Give them frequent opportunities to burp if they need to. (How's that for an opportunity for fun!) Be aware of possible discomfort in their ears, and be sure to drain and dry the ears thoroughly when they get out of the water.

- **Deal with hunger after swimming.** This hunger has a physiological reason. Water draws heat from your body faster than air does. Your child's body uses energy to keep warm, and the heat loss triggers their body to create insulation in the form of fat. Both of these things send a message to their brain that their body needs fuel.

    Also, swimming, like any other exercise, makes your child thirsty, but because they're not sweating—or at least aren't aware of sweating—they can become dehydrated without realizing it. Some of what your child perceives as hunger when they get out of the pool may actually be thirst.

    Have a warm drink ready for your child as soon as they get out of the pool, even on a hot summer day. (And how fun is that! You get the fun of hot chocolate or warm apple cider when it's not the season for it.) It will help them warm up and satisfy any thirst that's masquerading as hunger. After that, give them a snack.

- **Give your child plenty of recovery time.** It's important for your child's body and mind. Make sure your child gets rest—whether they want it or not—after a strenuous session in the pool.

Kids' feelings

The sensory experience of being in the water, as well as emotional associations, leads to a range of feelings your child might have about swimming. Be on the lookout for emotional distress that you can soothe and for opportunities to motivate your child.

Fear

It's never too early to help your child feel comfortable in the water. Younger kids—three and four years old—are less fearful than older kids—seven or eight years old—who are being introduced to the water for the first time.

Where does the fear come from?

- Fear of drowning can come from experience—like having slipped under the water in the tub for a moment—or from peers or the media.

- Fear can come from feelings of being out of control, confused or uncertain, powerless, or unsupported in the water.

- Fear can come from picking up parents' own fear, worry or concerns.

- For some kids, new things are scary.

Being afraid is reasonable. Until your child has the skills of water safety, the water is a dangerous place. That's the whole point. That's why they need to learn to swim.

How to address fear

Many actors feel stage fright before a performance. A common tool for getting past this fear is to reframe it as excitement. You can help your child by using this technique. Understand the fear. Address it. Reframe it as excitement.

First, talk to your child to try to isolate the reason for the fear. Next, address their concerns. If they're afraid that they'll slip and swallow water, explain that you'll be holding them and won't let that happen. If they fear the unknown, explain to them what to expect once they're in the water, from how it will feel to what you'll be doing and how long you'll do it. Watch YouTube videos together of kids and adults having fun in the water. (Make sure you prescreen what you watch so that you're sure there won't be any scary surprises.)

Once you've addressed their concerns, point out the physical signs of fear that they might be experiencing: increased heart rate, fast or shallow breathing, shivers, tension, a rush of adrenaline. All of those are things that also happen when you're excited. Have your child focus on what they're feeling in their body and how they've felt those same things when they've been excited about something. Associate the two feelings. It's hard to stay afraid when you're aware that your body is responding the same way it does when you wake up on the morning of your birthday party.

Anger

Your child might be angry at being forced to do something they don't want to do. They might feel anger about feeling afraid. They might feel anger in the form of frustration about not being able to physically control their body in the water as well as they'd like to be able to.

How to address anger

If they're angry at being forced to do something they don't want to do, give them as many choices as possible. "Would you like to go swimming and then to the park or to the park and then swimming?" or "Would you like to swim for fifteen minutes or for twenty minutes?"

If they're angry about feeling afraid, help them to express the anger and then address the fear.

If they're frustrated about not having the same degree of control over their movement in the water as they do on land, remind them that it took a lot of practice to learn to walk and to learn to run. Tell them funny stories about those early days. Scale back the skill you're working on to give them a break from the frustration and an opportunity to enjoy practicing something that they're already competent doing.

Happiness

Spending time playing in the water with your parents in the warm sun is fun. Don't gloss over the joy you and your child can share because you're in a rush to get to the next skill. The spaces between learning new things will be filled with the laughter that becomes memories your child will carry with them for the rest of their life.

Security

Your child will rely on you to set the tone for your time in the pool. If you feel confident and if you provide physical and emotional support, your child will feel secure. That sense of security will make them receptive to what you're trying to teach and will color their long-term feelings about swimming and the water.

Pride

As your child's efforts pay off and they learn new things and master new skills, they're likely to feel proud. Help to encourage and validate that feeling. Talk about how well they're doing to other adults in front of them. Give them a forum for sharing that pride.

Kids' motivation

Put yourself in your child's place. Why learn to do this? For some kids, watching older kids and seeing the potential fun is strong motivation. Kids who don't have an example like that might be harder to motivate. If you can have a great time running around on land, what's the point of working hard to learn to swim? What's in it for them?

On the other hand, the downsides of learning to swim are apparent from the beginning. The water's cold and uncomfortable. Sometimes it smells like chlorine. There may be strangers swimming in the pool. Your kid knows they wouldn't know what to do if they got in too deep, and that's legitimately scary. There's a sense of not having control or feeling in charge of the next moment. There are potentially uncomfortable sensations. Being in the water doesn't feel like being on land. There's the possibility of swallowing water—which probably doesn't taste very good—or getting water in their nose. That possibility quickly becomes uncomfortable and possibly scary reality, because it's hard to learn to swim without ever swallowing water or getting water in your nose.

Kids spend countless hours practicing new skills. They're relentless. They learn to roll over, sit up, crawl—sometimes backwards, it's true—walk, and run. These are all driven by another motive. Your child doesn't want to crawl for crawling's own sake. They want to get somewhere. They want to walk so they can get there faster. Run? Get there faster!

Other forms of movement require different motivation. Some kids (who may be great walkers or runners) may be lousy at skipping or climbing. Why? Where's the benefit in the movement for them? Swimming is like this. There's got to be either benefit that comes from the movement or pleasure in the movement itself.

You can highlight and set up benefits from the movement. If a game that relies on mastery of a skill is fun enough, your child will work at mastering that skill. If other kids your child admires are doing something, your child will work to do what it takes to join them or be like them. Go to the pool when other, older kids are there. Play games as a family. Show your child the possibilities that are waiting for them once they're able to swim.

You can use external motivation, depending on what's important to your child. Will they work for ribbons or gold stars? How about for a special activity together? Cold, hard cash? External motivation can help get your child over any bumps in the learning road when the experience of swimming isn't enough to motivate them on its own.

You can help your child enjoy the movement itself by pointing out the pleasurable sensations of being in the water and doing what you can to minimize the negative sensations. Make sure to help your child notice the way the water feels against their skin and the weightlessness of buoyancy. Make sure to keep them as warm as possible and to help them drain their ears. These small aspects of enjoying the movement and the water will help to motivate your child to keep getting back into the pool.

Kids' perceptions of success

Kids drop out of sports if they're not having fun and don't think they're doing well. In a study of 8- to 13-year-olds, the kids' opinions of what made a good swimmer had everything to do with effort: if you're trying your hardest, you're good. Kids care about the process more than the outcome. So as kids see it, "doing well" has a lot to do with trying your hardest.

Defining success based on process instead of outcome will help your child to remain engaged and feel successful. Emphasizing the importance of practice for improvement fits their efforts don't seem to be bringing them closer to mastery. Even when it doesn't look like they're making progress, their body is processing the experience. When they're not seeing results, reminding them that their brain, muscles, and nervous system are like secret agents doing work that won't be revealed right away is a good way to keep motivation levels high. You want to keep them motivated so they keep putting in the effort until the results show.

Kids' abilities

Think of what your child is capable of on land. If your baby is just learning to crawl, they'll be able to similarly explore moving their body in the water, but don't expect mastery. If your child can walk and run with great coordination, you can expect them to develop similar coordination in the water with practice. Keep your expectations reasonable.

Think about how much practice it took on land to develop the level of mastery your child has, though. Remember the process of learning to crawl, walk or run. At the beginning, it looked awkward and ungainly. Only with time and lots of practice did those movements become a natural way for your child's body to move. Swimming will be the same. So keep your expectations reasonable.

Good form will help your child swim farther and faster, but their body might not be capable of good form. Swimming is like dance, tennis, or golf. Kids learn quickly, but until their minds and bodies are developed enough, don't expect them to have the level of mastery you'd see in an adult. Did I mention that you should keep your expectations reasonable?

Athletes practice for a long time thinking about and practicing good form. At some point, it becomes second nature—internalized. Without thinking about it, they continue to improve. Learning to swim involves thinking and feeling in a very conscious way for a long time, and there's a lot to think about and a lot to feel. At some point, the knowledge starts to move into your child's body instead of just their head, just like walking or riding a bike.

Recent studies have pointed out that the amount of practice required to achieve mastery of a skill is ten thousand hours. And that's not just hours spent phoning it in; that's hours spent in mindful, specific, pinpoint-precision practice. It would take your child many years to get that much practice. Have you spent ten thousand hours of your life swimming? That's an hour a day for almost thirty years. In the meantime (you know what's coming!), keep your expectations reasonable.

Have I driven you crazy with the "keep your expectations reasonable" mantra? I've repeated it because it's so important. The way your child feels about swimming will depend in large part on your feelings and your feedback. If your expectations are reasonable, you'll feed their motivation to keep trying. If your expectations are unreasonable, you'll be frustrated, they'll be frustrated, neither of you will have any fun, and they'll want to stay out of the pool and quit rather than disappoint you.

Kids' abilities by age

6-18 months

When your child is six to eighteen months old, you can make sure they get a lot of exposure to the water, you can provide supported movement, and you can teach about water safety. Don't expect independent swimming or independent water safety.

18-36 months

When your child is a year and a half to three years old, they may be able to move themselves in the water. Don't expect fancy strokes. You can emphasize water safety, but don't expect them to be independently water safe.

Kids this age are big fans of the words "no" and "why." Use that to your advantage. Your child can follow instructions if you give them one at a time. They'll tend to get frustrated easily. Kids this age can usually throw or kick a ball well enough to move it a little, but they won't have real ability. They might be able to ride a tricycle, walk down stairs, run well, and stack blocks. Think of how your child throws a ball when you're working with them on moving their arms in the water.

Three to five years

When your child is three to five years old, they'll be able to achieve water safety. Keep in mind that this is not a substitute for adult supervision. No one of any age should swim alone. You can get to the point where you could describe your child as water safe and as being able to swim. At this point, your child might be able to do rudimentary versions of formal strokes.

Kids this age know a lot of words. They're aware of other kids and love to watch and be with other kids. They can run, gallop and dance. They're really good now at riding a tricycle and might even be able to ride a bike. They're better at throwing. They start understanding games and rules. You can use swimming with other kids as motivation to keep practicing, and you can use games in the water to help your child practice skills without the practice feeling like work.

Six years old

At six, your child can develop more precise movements and mastery of strokes.

Kids at this age are much more coordinated. They're good at skipping, throwing, and maybe catching. Their fine and gross motor skills are well developed. Other kids their age become an important part of their lives. At this stage, you'll start to see swimming that resembles somewhat coordinated strokes.

Seven and eight years old

Kids this age are often very curious. They've become good communicators. They have a strong sense of fair play. They can learn rules, and they do well with developing and practicing skills. They're learning to cope with frustration.

They'll also be likely to be afraid of the water if they haven't had experience with it before. They'll need a lot of time and a gradual approach to get past this fear.

9 years old and up

Kids this age are usually very coordinated and are good at listening and evaluating.

Adolescents

Kids this age are adjusting to the changes in their bodies' shape and distribution of weight. It can be an awkward time to learn new physical skills. Your normally graceful child might suddenly start bumping into things. Differences in individual athletic ability become more pronounced.

Whatever their age, your awareness of your child's body, sensory experience of the water, feelings, perceptions of success, motivation, and abilities should inform how you plan your lessons and carry them out.

Chapter 3
Getting a Head Start

You'll have a head start if you understand some underlying ideas about how kids learn in general, how they learn physical skills, how feelings can help you, and some key characteristics of swimming.

How kids learn

Learning a skill has several stages. First, you have to think about it, or get the idea of what you're learning. Next, you have to practice it until you can do it. Finally, you have to master it to the extent that you can not only do it without thinking but also adapt it to other situations. This process isn't always smooth or sequential.

Technique, the amount and consistency of practice, and attitude are the four things that contribute to how quickly and well your child learns to swim. Little things add up. The right things done consistently and carefully are cumulative.

You can help your child by teaching technique, by setting up a schedule that gives your child regular practice in manageable amounts, and by creating an atmosphere that's fun, with awareness of your child's physical and emotional needs.

Kids learn by playing

When kids—and adults, for that matter—play, they explore situations beyond what they've actually experienced, develop problem-solving skills, and create new neural networks. When they're creating huge towers out of blocks, they're learning physics. When they play princess or imagine being cats, they're learning sociology and psychology. When they play with plants or bugs, they're learning biology. They're also learning how to think, they're learning about themselves and other people, and they're creating friendships with the people they play with. Playing is a safe way for the brain to learn, because you can use your imagination without risk.

You can take advantage of this by using your imagination to create games and ways of looking at the lessons you're teaching that turn them into play. You can make improving form a game. There are lots of specific ideas in Chapter 11, but this is also a chance for you yourself to play and for you to play with your child.

Kids learn by figuring it out themselves

Kids learn best by thinking and solving problems. When kids figure things out themselves, they remember what they learn better and longer. Help and encourage your child to explore, and point them gently in the directions that will be more useful to them.

Kids learn in short spurts

Kids can focus intensely, but their attention spans aren't as long as adults' attention spans. Short and frequent lessons are better than long, occasional sessions. If you have easy access to a pool, two or three fifteen- or twenty-minute lessons a day would be ideal. (Don't worry, three fifteen-minute lessons a week will yield progress, too. It just won't be as fast.)

Kids need lots of practice

Practice is key. Studies have shown that complete mastery of a skill takes around ten thousand hours of precisely designed practice, adjusted based on the most specific attention to what needs the most work. Most of our kids won't achieve this level of mastery in their swimming even as adults, but each hour of practice brings them that much closer to the level of skill they need to be safe and confident in the water.

Provide as much opportunity to practice as possible, and make sure that a good chunk of that is unstructured.

Kids sometimes get stuck

Plateaus are normal. So are setbacks. Sometimes increased awareness of what's going on can actually make performance worse for a while, but that awareness is critical. It's part of the learning process.

Your child might get frustrated or discouraged at this point and want to stop trying. At first, they weren't aware of the mistakes they were making. Now that they've got more awareness, they're able to focus on the mistakes they were making before but just didn't notice. Encourage them and let them know that the experience is part of getting better. It's the perfect time to incorporate a game into practice.

How kids learn physical skills

Muscles learn by doing. Practice is important not only because your mind needs to understand what's happening but also because your muscles turn repeated motion into reflexive action.

Learning a physical skill, including swimming, is all about listening to your body and getting a feel for the water. There are four key aspects to what your child is learning in the water. They're learning about how their own body moves. They're learning about spatial relationships. They're learning about how much effort is required to produce different results or movements. They're learning about the relationship of the water to all of the other things—their body, space, and effort.

Athletes practice for a long time thinking about their form. At some point, form becomes natural—internalized. Without thinking about it, they continue to improve. When kids learn to swim, the process is very conscious for a long time, and there's a lot to think about and a lot to feel. At some point, the knowledge starts to move into your child's body instead of their head, just like walking or riding a bike.

If you've ever played a musical instrument, you've experienced this. You can play a piece of music you memorized years ago just by putting your hands on your instrument, but when you try to consciously remember what to play next, the ability slips away. This level of automatic proficiency comes to your child's swimming after enough practice.

Don't believe me? Try consciously thinking about what your body should do next the next time you go for a walk or run or ride a bike. Let me know if you can do it.

Feelings matter

Kids learn best when they feel safe and supported, physically and emotionally. If you feel relaxed and confident and you're having fun, it will be easier for your child to feel relaxed and confident and have fun.

Tension in your child's body makes it harder to learn a physical skill. Emotional tension makes it harder to retain and process information. It's up to you to create an atmosphere of fun, freedom, and exploration to help your child feel secure enough to learn.

According to a recent study of eight- to thirteen-year-old kids, kids' opinions of what makes a good swimmer have everything to do with effort: if you're doing your best—trying hard and practicing—you're good. Kids care about the process more than the outcome.

Defining success based on the process instead of outcome will help kids to remain engaged and feel successful. Feeling successful will make them want to keep trying. Emphasizing the importance of practice for improvement fits how kids think about things and gives them control over their own success.

Swimming

These five characteristics of swimming make learning to swim unlike the land-based skills your child already knows.

Finesse

Swimming isn't about brute strength. It's about finesse. It's not what you've got; it's how you use it. The better your child gets at swimming with good form, the less effort they'll need to swim farther, faster.

Your child knows that they can run faster if they up their effort. You'll need to help them understand that swimming better, not harder, will improve their performance.

Rhythm

Coordinating the movement of all the parts of the body in relationship to each other is key to swimming comfortably. Your child already knows how to do this intuitively if they can run. If they can skip, throw a ball, or kick, they're beginning to understand this concept in a more conscious way. In swimming, the rhythm of movement determines whether you move at all—in any direction—in a way that it doesn't on land.

Power

Most of the power in swimming comes from the arms, the core, and the hips. The rhythm of the movement makes it work. Kicking provides stability but not much propulsion.

This is exactly the opposite of land-based activities like running and biking, where the legs and core provide the power and the arms are secondary.

Drag

There's much less resistance when you move your body through air than there is when you move through water, so reducing drag is more important in swimming than it is in land-based activities. Any part of your body that's moving forward should be slicing through the water, disturbing it as little as possible. Any part of your body that's moving backwards should be maximizing resistance, using the water to push or pull against.

Relaxation

A big shift in skill and ability will happen when your child learns to relax in the water. Ironically, it's hard to relax in the water until you have enough skill to feel comfortable. You can help them by providing all the support they need, by feeling comfortable in the water yourself, and by letting them feel how comfortable you are.

You can also help with relaxation by making sure to introduce skills slowly, especially at first. The more you can make each lesson feel easy, the more you'll help your child feel like swimming lessons are no big deal—just another fun part of the day.

Ease

Nowhere is the concept of going with the flow clearer than in the water. It's easier to go with the flow than against the flow of the water. It's also more efficient and effective. In swimming, making it feel easier is good. If you feel like you're trying really hard, there's a good chance your movement is counterproductive.

The big picture

Keep these concepts in mind as you plan your lessons and as you spend time in and out of the pool with your child. Using these fundamentals to inform how you teach will allow your child to have the best, smoothest, fastest learning experience.

Chapter 4
Safety First

There's no substitute for common sense. The thought you put into preparing your environment, yourself, and your child for swimming is irreplaceable.

Since the Red Cross began working to teach water safety skills more than a hundred years ago, drowning deaths have dropped dramatically. Teaching your child to swim is one way to help keep them safe. Here are guidelines that also contribute to keeping them safe.

The environment

Whether you're swimming in your own pool, a friend's pool, a community pool, a lake, a river, or the ocean, knowing your environment and making it as safe as possible is the first step in keeping you and your child safe.

Weather

Know weather conditions and forecasts before you go swimming.

Don't go into the water—including the shower at the pool—during a thunderstorm. Go inside. Wait fifteen minutes after the thunder stops before going back into the water.

Don't go into the water in heavy rain or hail, during a tornado warning, or during high wind. High wind can make it harder to see—because of waves in the ocean—and can increase the risk of hypothermia even in a swimming pool.

Stay out of the water if fog is dense enough to interfere with visibility.

Pools

Whether you're at a friend's pool, a commercial pool, or your own pool, the following rules apply:

- Pools should be fenced or, where applicable, covered with an approved power locking cover. Keep the gate leading to the pool closed.

- Make sure that there's a working phone near the pool and that emergency numbers are posted.

- Don't use a pool or hot tub without a drain cover. Lack of a drain cover creates a significant drowning risk.

- Don't use glass of any kind around the pool. Be aware of things made of glass other than the obvious drinking glasses.

If you have a pool, check with your local building and planning department about safety standards in your community.

Barriers and alarms

Barriers and alarms aren't foolproof safeguards. They're designed to give you a little more time to look for a missing child before the child can accidentally—or with some effort—get into the pool. They're not a substitute for supervision.

If you have a pool, install a four-sided pool fence that's at least six feet high, with self-closing, self-latching, outward-opening gates and latches higher than kids can reach. Fences need to prevent kids from getting over, under or through them. They shouldn't have anything a child could use as a foothold or handhold for climbing. The U.S. Consumer Product Safety Commission (www.cpsc.gov) provides detailed information about the specific structure of fences.

Consider getting an alarm that sounds when the gate to the pool area opens. Make sure the switch for the alarm is locked or out of reach of kids.

A power—not manually operated—safety cover that meets ASTM standards (www.astm.org) can be used as a layer of protection, but remember that a young child can drown in just inches of water. A pool cover that sinks slightly below the surface of the water or that has puddles on it can be a drowning hazard even if it prevents a child from getting into the pool.

Around the pool

Don't use breakable tabletops, lamps, vases, or other furnishings around the pool.

Remove steps and ladders from aboveground pools when the pool isn't being used.

Don't leave tempting toys in or near the water. Remove them from the pool area when you're not there. Kids can fall into the pool while they're trying to reach a toy.

The pool itself

Have your pool inspected regularly. Know and clearly mark the electrical cut-off switch for the pool pump.

Install a Safety Vacuum Release System, which shuts off the drainage pump if the drain is blocked, preventing kids from becoming trapped at the bottom of the pool by the suction of the drain on their hair, clothing, or part of their bodies.

Keep the water level of the pool high enough to make it easy for a small child to reach the edge of the pool and pull himself out.

Open water

If you're going to swim in open water, be prepared and educate yourself. Swim where there's a lifeguard on duty. The US Lifesaving Association reports that you're five times more likely to drown at a beach without a lifeguard.

Don't float (using a flotation device) where you can't swim. The exceptions to this are in a lifejacket in an emergency situation and when your child is wearing one in a pool while you supervise.

If you're going to swim in the ocean, educate yourself. Know the ocean, especially rip tides. Don't fight the current. If you get caught in a rip tide, swim parallel to it until you reach its edge, then turn toward shore. Know and obey beach warning flags.

Use a US Coast Guard-approved life jacket when boating, no matter what. Being a good swimmer is critical in a disaster, but it may not be enough to keep you safe in rough conditions, over long periods of time, or if you lose consciousness.

Behavior

There's no substitute for common sense. Make sure you know basic safety rules and procedures and that your kids do, too. Then follow those rules and procedures. When in doubt, err on the side of caution.

Preparation

Don't wait for the moment an emergency happens to plan for it.

- Learn to swim.

- Learn CPR.

- Before you get into the water, make sure you know where to find a phone. Make sure that phone is working.

- Before you get into the water, make sure you know where to find emergency phone numbers.

- Before you get into the water, make sure you know where to find the emergency shut-off for the pool pump.

- Before you get into the water, evaluate your surroundings.

- Wear sunscreen and, if necessary, protective clothing. Reapply sunscreen frequently. Make sure that clothing you wear to protect yourself from the sun is designed to act as sun protection. Don't wear cotton to protect yourself from the cold and wet. Instead, choose fabrics with better insulating properties.

Kids

Show your child where the pool rules are posted and explain them. Quiz them. Ask them to teach you the rules. Review them every time you arrive at the pool until they're second nature to your child.

Don't be afraid to explain safety risks to your child. Be calm and direct. You don't want to make them unnecessarily afraid of the water, but you do want them to respect it and the safety rules. Explain what behavior is unsafe, why it's dangerous, and how to choose different safe behaviors.

Set an example for your child. If kids aren't allowed to jump in, neither should you.

In the same way that kids' bodies lose heat rapidly in a cold pool, they can overheat quickly in a hot tub. Hyperthermia can cause weakness, dizziness, confusion, and loss of consciousness. Your child may experience the effects of the heat well before an adult would.

Never throw your child into the water to teach them to swim. It's not safe, and it won't teach them to swim.

When your child feels comfortable in shallow water, watch to make sure they don't move to deeper water than is safe for their skill level. Kids like to use the wall to move and like to bounce. Both of these can accidentally take them to deeper water than they can handle.

The two most serious water injuries are drowning and spinal injuries. Most spinal injuries result from dives in shallow water. Always make sure you know how deep the water is before diving. Don't let your child dive in any way in water that's less than six feet deep. Don't let your child dive headfirst in any water that's less than nine feet deep, or twelve feet deep if your child is diving from a board.

Supervision

It takes only 20 seconds for a child to drown.

Always supervise your child when they're in and around the water, even if they're wearing a flotation device. Flotation devices can provide a false sense of confidence for parents and kids. They're meant for emergencies, not as a substitute for supervision.

Even if your kids are water safe, supervise them. No one should swim alone, and kids shouldn't ever swim without adult supervision.

Designate an adult supervisor, and make sure everyone knows who that person is. Ideally that person should have lifeguard, first aid, and CPR training. The adult should be focused on watching the kids. If you takes shifts, make sure everyone acknowledges that they understand whose shift it is.

Kids drown without making noise. The cartoon image of a drowning victim splashes, yells, and comes up a few times before finally sinking slowly below the surface. That's not how it works with kids. They fall in with the noise of one small splash. They go under. They don't come up again.

When you're watching kids in and around the water, remember:

- Eliminate distractions. Don't talk on the phone or text. Don't read or watch TV. Don't do yard work or fold laundry.

- Don't divide your attention by supervising kids who *aren't* in or around the pool while you're also supervising kids who *are* in or around the pool.

- Keep talks brief and keep your eyes on your responsibility.

- Don't eat.

- Don't drink alcohol.

- If you need to leave the pool area for any reason, even for a few seconds, make sure all of the kids are safely out of the pool and pool area while you're away.

Babysitters should also know the risks and procedures.

Grownups, too

Adults need to pay attention to their own safety, too.

- Don't swim alone. Swim with a friend.

- Don't drink while swimming (or doing other water activities like boating or waterskiing) or supervising kids.

- Don't use inflatable armbands or other toy-like flotation devices in place of life jackets.

- Don't dive in shallow water or in water of unknown depth. Spinal injuries from diving into shallow water are common in both kids and adults.

- Don't run on the pool deck. It can be slippery, which makes falling likely. It's a hard enough surface to hurt you badly. That combination of slippery and hard could knock you unconscious and send you flying into the pool, so it's a drowning risk, too. Walk on the deck instead of running.

In case of emergency

In any emergency, call your emergency number immediately. (911 in the United States.)

If your child is missing, always look in the pool before you look anyplace else. A child can drown in twenty seconds. Scan the surface and the bottom of the pool. Search the area around the pool next. If you leave the pool area to continue searching, make sure the pool area is secure before you leave. A wandering child could return to the pool and fall in after you've searched there.

If someone is trapped at the pool's drain, turn off electrical power right away, before you do anything else. Don't try to pull the person directly from the suction. Instead, break the suction's seal by prying between the person's body and the suction, with your hand if necessary.

Chapter 5
Before You Start

If you'll be making a lot of trips to the pool, do yourself a favor and put together a kit of supplies you'll take with you every time you go. Make a list and keep it with your pool kit. Check the list before you go to the pool, and replenish the supplies when you get home.

Preparation for getting into the pool

Before you get into the pool, gather the toys, equipment and clothing you'll need, and plan what you'll do.

Toys and equipment

Depending on what skills you'll be practicing, you might want to bring toys that will help you to teach. They can be specialized, or they can just be things you have around the house.

Washcloths and hand towels are great for providing a cool, comfortable place for your child to sit on the edge of the pool. They're also good for games. Coins serve not only as something to retrieve from the bottom of the pool but also as built-in motivation to retrieve it.

Foam noodles and rings for the pool can be great teaching tools, but you can also use toys that aren't designed specifically for swimming, such as regular balls and other toys. Just make sure you know which ones float and which ones sink. Dog toys are great for kids to play with in the pool. They come in a huge variety of sizes and fun shapes.

Whatever objects you use, make sure that they're appropriate for your child's developmental level.

Tools like kickboards, inflatable armbands, and fins can be useful for getting kids to feel comfortable and confident in the water, but they also have downsides:

- They can give your child too much confidence. You don't want to experience the moment when your child, not yet water safe, jumps into the pool because they forgot that they didn't have their armbands on.

- They don't teach kids to swim. Being in the water without one of these tools doesn't feel the same as being in the water with them; time spent using them isn't helping with actual swimming skills.

- They can become a crutch. If you don't ditch them early enough in the learning process, your child will start to feel uncomfortable in the water without them and won't be willing to give them up easily.

What to wear

Apply sunscreen liberally twenty minutes or so before you get into the pool. Don't forget to apply sunscreen yourself. Not only is it good for you, but also it makes your child more willing to accept the application when it's their turn. You might also consider having your child wear a long-sleeved T-shirt that's designed for sun protection over their swimsuit.

If you do have them wear a T-shirt, choose a synthetic fabric designed to dry quickly, not cotton. Cotton becomes heavy when it's wet. It can also become rough and uncomfortable to the skin when it's wet. It does nothing to keep you warm in the water, and once you get out of the water, a wet cotton T-shirt will continue to draw heat from your body, keeping you as cold as if you'd remained in the pool.

Consider a wet suit if the pool is cool. Kids lose body heat faster than adults. Most pools are kept at 70 to 80 degrees F. The ideal pool temperature for kids is at least 80 degrees F, preferably warmer. For infants, the pool must be very warm, around 95 degrees F.

If your child will wear them, they'll be more comfortable learning to swim if they wears goggle. They're great for protecting their eyes from the pool chemicals and for helping them adjust to putting their head under the water.

You can have your child practice wearing goggles on dry land and in the swimming pool. If they're already used to wearing goggles before they get into the pool for the first time, they'll have one fewer new thing to adjust to. Plus, nothing's more hilarious than when everyone wears swimming goggles at the dinner table.

Don't wear sunglasses. You want to be able to have good eye contact with your child. If you need to shield your eyes from the sun, choose a baseball cap or another hat with a brim.

Things to do

Check with your child's doctor to make sure your child's health allows them to start learning to swim. Consider getting a physical yourself. Don't go swimming if you have GI upset, an infected cut, poison oak, a rash, a fever, a contagious illness, pink eye, an earache, or a cold with green or yellow mucus.

Schedule pool time when your child won't need a nap and there won't be loud noises or lots of distractions.

Don't eat for an hour before swimming. Your mom was right. Your body needs time to digest. Acidic foods in particular can combine with the new physical experiences of swimming and the likelihood of swallowed pool water to lead to an upset stomach.

Familiarize yourself with the pool. How deep is it? Where does the depth change and how deep does it get?

Plan your approach before you get into the pool. Have a list of activities you want to try and the equipment you'll need for those activities. Plan more than you actually expect to be able to do, so that you'll have the flexibility to try new things if what you try first isn't working. Write your lesson plan on an index card and put it into a waterproof plastic bag. Read your lesson plan and refer to it during the lesson if you need to.

Right before you get into the pool, have your child go to the bathroom, blow their nose, and spit gum or food into the trash. You might as well take care of these things for yourself, too, while you're at it. If you have to get out of the pool to use the bathroom during your lesson, your child will have to get out, too, and they'll probably be cold and unwilling to get back into the pool.

Keep your eye on the clock. It's always better to leave them wanting more.

Preparation for getting out of the pool

Go straight from the pool to the shower after swimming. Kids' skin is especially sensitive to pool chemicals.

Don't forget to have towels, a warm drink—even if it's hot out—and a snack ready for right after your lesson. Swimming requires a lot of energy. Aside from all of the energy it takes to swim, there's also a big energy expenditure just maintaining normal body temperature, even in a warm pool.

It's a good idea to have more than one towel for your child. If the towels are big and fluffy, that's even better. Spread your towels out so that the sun warms them while you're in the pool. Use one towel to wrap around your child's body while you use another to thoroughly dry their head and ears.

Make sure to drain their ears and dry them well. Fluid trapped in the ear can be a breeding ground for outer ear infections. Have your child tilt their head from side to side to drain their ears. You can also use a blow dryer on the low setting to gently warm the air next to their ears.

Chapter 6
Your First Time at the Pool

You've got all your gear ready to go. You're well rested, and so is your child. You've read this book, learned how to teach and what to teach. You're in the car and ready to go. What now? First, make sure you've got the kid in the car with you. No? Back into the house for them then. Okay, ready?

Take it slow. Enjoy each other. Have fun. If you don't enjoy each other and have fun, it's going to be hard—maybe impossible—for you to teach your child to swim. Your first visit to the pool will set the tone for the lessons to come. Use what you know about your child to make it a great experience for them and they'll be happy to come back again and again.

When you get there

When you get to the pool, show your child where the pool rules are posted and explain them, even if they can't read yet. Make sure they understand never to go near or into the pool without an adult. Make sure they understand not to run in the pool area and not to jump or dive (unless the pool is deep enough and the rules allow it).

Show them where the bathroom is. (You'll be needing it before you get into the pool, anyway.) Check to see if there are any cool insects around, if they're that age and that's their thing. Ease into it.

What kind of learner is your child? Do they like to observe from a distance? Do they like to jump right in? Respect their learning style.

If your child likes to observe before experiencing something for themselves, this is the perfect opportunity to sit near the pool together and let them watch other kids playing. If your kid likes to jump into things right away, by all means get in the pool. Don't rush things here, though. Spending the first day just watching other kids have fun is a good use of your time. If your child doesn't even get their toes wet, that time hasn't been wasted.

The lesson plan for your first lesson: let your child watch and explore. Don't plan a formal lesson for the first visit. If it takes a few visits for your child to feel comfortable getting in the pool, don't plan a formal lesson for the first time they actually get into the pool, either.

Don't force your child to get into the pool, and don't let disappointment or disapproval color your interactions. This is for your child. It needs to happen at their pace. You can encourage your child to get in or to participate in play if you sense that they secretly kind of wants to, but don't pressure them. If there's another adult available to supervise your child, you can set an example by playing in the water while your child sits outside the pool and watches you. Provide encouragement, support, and time.

Getting in

If your child does want to try getting into the pool, seat them on the edge of the pool. Keep a hand on them while you climb into the pool first. Making sure you're stable, stand facing your child, and use both arms to transfer them from the edge of the pool into a close hug. Keep your head and your child's head close together and at the same level to help them feel secure.

Splash together, play together, and explore the feel of the water together. Don't give in to the temptation to start a lesson. This visit is just for getting used to the water.

When your child is first getting used to the water, try to avoid splashing their face with water. Instead, get their face wet gently, by stroking them with your fingers. If their face does get wet, don't wipe it off. There's nothing wrong with getting a little wet, so don't send a non-verbal message that says otherwise.

Don't push practice too long. Not only does it stop being fun, but also it's physically less effective. If your child is tired, everything will feel harder and scarier.

The most important thing

After safety, the most important thing to accomplish on your first visit is to have fun. You're not just introducing your child to the water. You're also introducing them to the style and approach you'll take when you're teaching them to swim, setting up their expectations for how they'll feel about spending time in the pool with you, and setting in motion the development of feelings they'll have toward swimming for the rest of their life. If it's not fun, step back, adjust your expectations for yourself and your child, and try for fun again. Not only will it help your child learn, it'll be…fun.

Chapter 7
How to Teach

Great teachers have fabulous insights into how kids think and feel, deep creative reservoirs to draw from when they plan lessons, keen instincts for interacting with kids and modifying lessons on the fly to make the most of each teachable moment, and years of experience. As your child's first teacher, you've already got these insights, creative reservoirs, instincts, and experience. You can make the most of your experience teaching your child to swim by honing and expanding on what you've already got.

If you've read Chapter 2, you've already heightened your insights into how kids think and feel. In Chapter 11, you'll get ideas for plumbing the depths of your creative well (and lots of ideas for when you feel like your well has run dry). You already have experience working with, playing with, and teaching your child.

Here you'll learn how to structure lessons, interact with your child to optimize how those lessons work, and adapt when there's an opportunity to get more out of your lesson.

The fundamentals

You can teach your child to be water safe in a way that's fun for both of you and intuitive for your child. In order to do it, you need to create an atmosphere that makes it easy to teach and easy to learn. You need to use a teaching style that supports that atmosphere. You need to structure lessons in a way that helps your child learn. You need to be attuned to your child. You need to make the most of your time in the water. You can also bring the lessons out of the pool in ways that a hired swimming teacher can't.

Creating the atmosphere

How you set the stage for your lessons will have a huge impact on how your child feels about it, and your child's attitude will determine whether they're willing and able to learn. Plan your lesson for a time when you're not rushed or tense. Your kids can sense tension in your face and body. They pick it up and become tense, too. You need to be truly relaxed.

Project confidence, calm, and enthusiasm. Make sure those feelings come through in your voice. Don't yell. Reassure your child with jokes, laughter, and hugs. Use a patient, nurturing, positive attitude. Remind yourself that making it fun isn't only an end in itself; it's also an important part of setting the stage for deep, thorough learning.

Having your own emotions on an even keel will help you respond to your child. If your child is afraid or nervous, point out how close those feelings are to excitement. The way you frame their experience for them will help shape how they perceive it. The physical sensations for a little kid trying to go to sleep the night before their birthday aren't far removed from the ones they feel when they're getting ready to try something new. Remind them about some of their favorite activities and how there was a moment in their life when they hadn't tried those activities yet. This could be the moment right before discovering a new favorite.

Be trustworthy. Be honest. Let your child know what to expect, and follow through. If you say you won't dunk them, don't dunk them. Your child needs to be able to trust you in the water so that they'll have enough confidence to take the risks learning to swim entails. If you break that trust, it will take a long time to regain it. It can make learning to swim very difficult, possibly even leading to a lifelong fear of the water. If you're a trustworthy teacher, your child will trust that they're safe in the water.

Don't expect your child to do it perfectly. Don't expect them to be fast or coordinated. Don't expect them to progress without setbacks or plateaus. If you start to get frustrated, take a break. You're not going to teach effectively when you're frustrated, your child won't learn anything, and you'll transfer your lousy mood and tension to them. Better to hop out of the pool for a few minutes and lie on your backs together watching for animals in the puffy clouds floating by.

Crafting a teaching style

When you're teaching, you and your child will work together to bring them understanding of each skill. You'll explain and demonstrate, but you'll also give them room to explore on their own. You'll need to learn to observe so that you'll not only be able to provide your child with the praise, constructive feedback, and physical guidance they need to help them "get it" when they're practicing but also to adapt your lesson plan based on your observations.

Explaining

Plan to teach one skill or one part of a skill at a time. For example, focus only on blowing bubbles to start. Focusing on more than one thing at a time is tough.

The first step in working with any skill is explaining what you'll be doing, in both simple and imaginative terms.

Fear

If your child expresses fear, try to reframe that fear as excitement and possibility. If that doesn't work, don't force them to try doing what they fear. Work towards it instead. Move on to demonstrating. Backtrack to practicing skills they've already mastered if necessary and come back to your explanation of the new skill from a new angle.

Imagination

Use imagination and visualization. In some ways, your body in the water is like a fish. In other ways, it's like a boat. In other ways, it's like a dancer. When you're completely submerged, you're like a fish. When you're swimming on the surface of the water, you're like a boat. When you're moving all of the parts of your body in coordinated motion, you're like a dancer or another athlete.

When fish swim, they're graceful. They're balanced. They're slippery. They move efficiently, with each motion propelling them through the water. A well designed boat slices through the water, creating as little resistance and drag as possible. Dancers and other athletes are aware of where each part of their body is in space.

As you approach each new skill, use these themes of a fish, a boat, and dancers and other athletes to help describe how the skill fits into the whole. If the ideas of fish, boats, dancers, and other athletes don't float your child's, um, boat, you can tailor your themes to incorporate your child's interests. Dancers are great examples of coordinated motion. So are baseball, basketball, soccer, and hockey players. Fish slip gracefully through the water, but so do mermaids.

Senses

Use all of your child's senses to teach. What does a skill look like, feel like, sound like? Maybe your child can even associate a taste or smell with a particular skill. The more hooks you can use to capture your child's attention and imagination, the more deeply they'll learn the skill.

Keep it simple

Once you've discussed the concepts in all sorts of imaginative ways, be prepared to boil down what you're asking your child to do into just one or two words. The background ideas of fish and boats are a foundation for their interest and understanding. The simple instruction to "blow bubbles" or kick with "knees straight" will help your child to focus in the moment on exactly what they need to do.

Demonstrating and setting an example

Making sure your child is safe—either fully supported by you in the pool or safely out of the pool—demonstrate the skill you've been talking about. Don't be tempted to bust a move and show off your spectacular swimming prowess at this point.

You want to make your child feel comfortable and capable. Demonstrate just the tiny piece you'll be focusing on. Tiny pieces that eventually can be pieced together are less intimidating and overwhelming than a complex skill demonstrated all at once.

You'll also be demonstrating to your child how they should feel about the water and their learning experience by how you react to what happens in the water. Don't overreact if they swallow some water. Instead, show them how to cough and blow their nose, and move on.

If water gets on your face or your child's face, don't wipe it off. Show them that it's okay to get water on their face by leaving it there or by making a game out of painting on each other's faces with the water that splashes from the pool. If you make it fun, your child will have fun.

Exploring

The more your child directs their own learning, the more engaged and ready to learn they'll be. Instead of directing them, involve them in the process of discovery. After you explain and demonstrate a skill, use questions and suggestions to guide them through the process.

This method of teaching is a little bit like being a journalist. Instead of asking yes/no questions, ask open-ended questions that give your child a chance to use their problem-solving skills. For example:

Instead of:

- Can you blow bubbles?

Try:

- If you were going to blow bubbles, how would you start?
- What's your favorite way to blow bubbles?
- Show me how to blow bubbles.
- Let's blow bubbles together.

You can give suggestions or clues to help. Instead of saying, "Touch the water with your lips," say, "What would happen if you touched the water with your lips?" or "How about trying to touch the water with your lips?"

Use games and imagination to reinforce and expand skills and to make repetition and practice interesting. Games and imagination engage the learner so that they practice without realizing it's practice, and fun distracts from fears and discomfort. Has your child ever told you they're hungry only at bedtime after the fun and activity of the day are finally over? Playing games and using imagination will help your child experience their lesson as a fun, flow-state activity. They'll want to stay in the pool and keep practicing, and they'll want to come back tomorrow.

Kids learn by playing. Plan ahead, choosing several games to try. If one doesn't interest your child, try another. When your child tries changing or expanding a skill you're practicing or a game you're playing, you might be tempted to narrow their focus. Don't. Encourage them to try things they initiate, as long as you're there to keep them safe.

Observing

Part of the process of learning is a feedback loop. You try something, watch how it's going, and adjust your approach accordingly. If you don't watch how what you're practicing is going, you risk practicing a skill the wrong way and making a habit of bad form.

Don't expect very young kids to learn strokes very well or to move quickly in the water. Think of how difficult other activities requiring coordination, such as throwing or kicking a ball, are for them. They're not going to look as polished as adults when they're little, no matter how much they practice. They're just not developmentally ready.

Your observations and feedback, though, can help your child to get the best feel for what they're doing and the best approximation of good form that they're ready to achieve.

While your child is practicing, watch them from the front, back, side, and underneath. Start by watching the whole body. Look for blips in the overall rhythm and unevenness in the sides of the body. Look to see if the major movements are flowing.

Next look at the smaller body parts involved in the movement, to see if they're supporting or working against the overall movement. Finally, watch parts of the body that aren't specifically involved in the practice.

Even when they're just blowing bubbles, you can look for tension in their arms and legs, so that you can help them relax. When they're practicing kicking, you can watch not only the overall movement, their feet, their hips, and their knees, but also the position of their head and the expression on their face. Use your peripheral vision to watch the quality of movement of the whole body when you're focusing on one body part. Even if you don't act on what you notice right away, the information you get from careful observation will be useful as your lessons progress.

Giving praise and support

Providing your child with support each step of the way can help them relax enough to move with patience and precision instead of frenetic energy.

Some kids respond well to frequent reinforcement. Others want you to keep out of their way. You know your child best. If you sense that they're confused, frustrated, or distracted, help them regain their focus by giving them feedback.

When you're praising your child's progress, be specific and constructive. General feedback such as "you're doing great" actually makes kids insecure about what they're doing. If they know they're doing great, but they don't know how or why, they tend to be afraid that they'll fail.

Instead, make your feedback as precise as you can. For example:

Instead of:

- Great job!

Try saying:

- I really like how hard you're trying.

- You're doing a really good job of flicking your foot when you kick.

Giving feedback and corrections

The same concept applies to corrections. Be as specific as possible. Saying, "come on, you can do better" makes your child feel inadequate without giving them any help in trying to do better.

You can give feedback while your child is practicing, or you can take a break to explain, depending on how complex the idea you need to express is.

Give the feedback immediately, so that what their body is doing or has just been doing is fresh in your child's mind and so that they know exactly what movement you're talking about. Break your feedback into steps.

Point out what is working.

- I really like how hard you're trying and how much attention you're paying to what you're doing.

Point out what isn't working.

- I notice that your knees are bending a lot while you kick.

Explain why it's not working or isn't the best approach.

- Your legs can push the water better if they stay straight.

Make suggestions and ask for suggestions for how to improve. Include physical feedback.

- Do you feel the air here when you kick? (At this point, you can touch your child's foot or calf.) One way to tell when you're keeping your legs straight is that you'll stopping feeling the cold air there.

- What ideas do you have about how to keep your legs straight?

- What ideas do you have about how you'll feel it when your legs are straight?

- Show me how you kick with your legs straight.

Follow up with more feedback.

- Your legs are really staying straighter now. The changes you made really worked.

After detailed feedback, you can use simple reminders as shorthand to remind your child of what you've already gone over together.

- Great effort. Knees straight.

Be sure to give one correction at a time. A list of things to work on is too overwhelming. If you notice several things that need work, pick the one that you think will make the biggest difference to work on first. After your child has gotten comfortable with one change to what they're doing, you can introduce the next.

If your child is having trouble with a skill, try having them exaggerate what they're doing wrong. For example, if they're not straightening their arm to take a stroke, have them purposely keep their arms bent and tight against their sides, so that they can really feel the problem.

Trying to do it wrong also lightens the mood. You not only want to give your child permission to fail, you want to encourage it. This creates an atmosphere of open exploration that will help your child to get a better understanding of their body's relationship to the water. It will also give them the freedom to risk trying new things, because they won't be afraid of the consequences of failure.

You can also try having them exaggerate what you're asking them to do. Try having them keep their knees perfectly straight for some practice kicks on the side of the pool. Even though this would never happen in actual swimming, getting a body feel for the extreme can help them move in the direction of good form.

Remember to use a patient, nurturing, positive attitude. Learning is a process. It's not always smooth or linear. Sometimes you need to try several approaches before you find one that works for your child or before what you're trying to teach them really "clicks." If you or your child start to get frustrated, take a break or switch to practicing another skill or playing a game.

Giving physical feedback

Take time during the lesson to point out the physical sensations. It usually takes ten or fifteen minutes for a repetitive physical sensation to really register with your brain and muscles, but you can suggest paying attention to the sensations any time along the way. You might think this is advanced for your child, but they was doing these things themselves when they learned to crawl, walk, and run.

Touch the part of your child's body that you want them to focus on. Touch their hip while explaining that that's where the movement of the kick comes from. Touch their thigh and explain that that's the muscle that will be doing most of the work.

You can use your hands to help adjust your child's body gently, guiding them to position themselves. Don't force them into position. If you feel resistance, don't try to push past it. Use gentle touch and words.

Going with the flow

Your ability to adapt your lesson plan to exactly what your child needs on any given day gives you a big advantage over swimming schools that have group lessons or college students teaching from a rote formula.

If your child says they're bored or looks bored, move on to something else even if you'd planned to spend more time on the current skill. It may be that they're approaching mastery of the skill at their level.

Take the feedback your child gives you, in words and in body language, about how they're experiencing the lesson. If they're tense or unhappy, ask them about it. Take a short break, play a game, or switch to a skill they've already mastered.

If your child seems fascinated by practicing a skill or exploring something new, and you'd planned to move on to something else, let them stick with it until they've exhausted their interest.

The plan you make for each lesson is a starting point. Let your child's responses to what you're teaching determine how closely you follow your plan. The more you follow your child's interests, the more they'll get out of the lesson, even if what they're learning isn't exactly what you thought it would be.

When you're learning to swim, you don't have the same level of control over your body and your life as when you're on land. That lack of control can be stressful or scary. The more you let your child control what's happening in the water, the more confidence they'll have and the more comfortable they'll feel about trying new things. The more new things they try, the more quickly they'll learn how their body works in the water. The better their understanding of how their body works in the water, the easier it will be to learn each new skill. Letting your child lead you away from your original lesson plan can make the entire process of learning to swim go more smoothly.

Structuring lessons

Prepare what you're going to teach well before you get to the pool. Make sure what you're planning to teach is a single skill. If you can break it down into simpler pieces, break it down and pick just one of the pieces to teach.

You can take advantage of the time you spend away from the pool to prepare your child for what the day's lesson will be. Over breakfast, you can talk about what you'll be learning, why it's important, and what's fun about it.

Lesson outline

- Explain to your child what you'll be doing
- Get into the pool
- Review what you've already learned
- Play
- Teach a new skill

- Practice the new skill

- Play

Lay the groundwork

Talk with your child about what you'll be doing. Ask your child what parts of the body they think they'll be focusing on or using most. Ask why it's important to learn the skill. Ask how they think it will feel. Ask what they think the favorite part of the lesson will be. Help them visualize how their body will move. Will they be moving like a fish? Like a boat? Tell them a story about the movement. Compare it to other animals or other activities they already know.

Practice any elements of the skill that you can on land. Blow bubbles in a bowl or sit on the edge of a chair to practice kicking.

Lay as much groundwork as you can for your lesson while you're at home, at the park, or out doing errands. That way, when you're at the pool, ready to start the lesson, you can use more of your valuable pool time just for learning and practicing, instead of for explaining.

Each lesson should last fifteen to twenty minutes. If your child appears happy to continue and comfortable in the water—not too cold or tired—you can spend as long as half an hour on your lesson.

Getting into the pool

After you've taken care of the pre-pool routine—making sure there's a working phone nearby, hitting the bathroom, spitting out gum or anything else in your mouths, and putting all of your post-pool equipment where you can get to it quickly when you're done—it's time to get into the pool.

Getting into the pool can be quick and easy or it can take most of your time, depending on where you and your child are in the process. Unless getting into the pool is the new skill you're teaching or is the recently learned skill that you're reviewing, take just a minute or two to get into the pool together.

Reviewing what you've already learned

Reviewing is the heart of the lesson. This is so important that I'll say it again: reviewing is the heart of the lesson. The first time your child is exposed to a new skill, they only scratch its surface. They have to listen to you, watch you, and feel their own body, all while trying to interpret your feedback and the feedback they're getting from their body and the water. It's a big job, and it's a lot to process. Not all of that processing is going to take place in the pool.

After you teach a new skill and get out of the pool, your child will rest and play and do other things, but they're still thinking about the skill you introduced. They're still getting insights into how it worked. They're still analyzing what was going on in the pool. A whole bunch of the learning of the new skill takes place after the lesson is over. They might even dream about it!

Don't be disappointed if the bulk of your lesson is dedicated to review. That's the way it's supposed to be. That's going to help your child really get it.

Don't expect your child to pick up where you left off at the end of the last lesson. Backtrack a bit and work up to the skills your child was working on at the end of the last lesson. If there are skills your child has already mastered, you don't need to work on them in every lesson. Start your review at the very beginning of the previous lesson's new material and spend five to ten minutes practicing it. If your child feels really confident after the first five minutes, you can move on. If they still seem tentative, use more of your lesson on review.

Try having your child experiment with doing the skill in different ways and comparing the results. Ask them to point out what they think works the best. Steer them away from unsafe or ineffective movements.

Ask your child how they think things are going. After some practice, make the skill a vehicle for play.

Playing

After you and your child have reviewed, spend just two or three minutes taking a break to play a game. This small break will signal that you've accomplished something and it will give your child a chance to relax and stretch, preventing them from overtiring one part of their body. It will also prime their mind and their mood for learning something new.

Present them with several suggestions of games that use the skill they've been practicing, and let them choose their favorite. They'll feel like they're taking a break and getting a treat, but really playing with the skill they've been practicing deepens their knowledge and understanding of the skill in ways that drills won't.

If things get out of hand and you end up playing so long that you don't have time to introduce something new, that's cause for celebration. Your child has been having fun, strengthening their body and their skills, and bonding with you. What could be better than that?

Teaching something new

Many parents want to spend most of their time in the pool working on something new. Instead, treat the introduction of the new skill as a preview of tomorrow's lesson. If your child still has a lot of room to learn more about the skill you've been reviewing, devote the whole lesson to review instead.

If you'll be teaching something new, choose a new skill that builds on something your child has already mastered. Make sure you choose a single step to work on. For example, if you're working on a new arm movement, don't try to add a new leg movement at the same time. The new skill should feel mildly challenging at most. If it feels hard, provide more support or back off and practice a slightly easier version of the same skill.

By the time you're in the pool, you've already discussed what you'll be doing. Give your child a brief reminder and start teaching. Remember to demonstrate what your child will be doing, let them explore, and give them praise and feedback. Take two or three minutes to have them learn the basic idea.

Once you're in the pool, try to narrow your verbal instructions down to just a couple of words. If you need to explain something in more depth, take a break so that your child doesn't have to divide their attention between listening to you and trying to do what you're asking them to do.

Practicing the new skill

With repetition, practice, and review, your child will turn the new movement they're learning into something habitual and ingrained that requires very little thought. In the early stages, though, each moment of what they're doing takes a lot of focus and attention. It's easiest for them to learn when they're fresh and their body and mind aren't too tired.

Depending on how long you've spent on getting into the pool, reviewing, playing, and teaching the new skill, you'll probably have between one and five minutes to practice. This may not seem like much, but remember that today's new skill is the skill you'll be reviewing at length in your next lesson. The important thing is to introduce the skill and give your child a chance to get a small taste of how it feels.

If your child gets frustrated, switch to a different approach to the same skill or to a different skill entirely. Look at what they're finding difficult and demonstrate it again. Touch their body to indicate where their focus should be. Have them touch your body while you demonstrate. Feeling their own ankle when it's flexed and pointed will be helpful, but seeing and feeling your ankle when it's flexed and pointed will give them a different perspective.

Acknowledge the small subtle things that are happening as your child practices. Point out how balance and buoyancy come into play, highlighting which parts of the body are more likely to sink and which parts are more likely to float. Talk about how their body moves and feels in the water. Keep it brief and to the point, just a touch and a "feel your knee?" while they're swimming is the most attention they can spare while they're also trying to practice moving. Save the details for later when you're on dry land.

Remember to progress from easy to difficult and from simple to complex:

- When you're working on floating, start with providing lots of physical support and progress to providing little or none.

- When you're working on a distance, start with short and work up to the width or length of the pool.

- When you start a skill, speed doesn't matter. Work up to being able to do it fast or at different speeds.

- When you start a skill, refine it slowly. At first, just doing it is enough. As you practice, work on refining body position, then movement, and then timing.

Playing (again!)

Working with your own child in the pool, you have the luxury of goofing off without having to worry that a paying parent will think you're shirking your teaching duties. You also have the important knowledge that playtime is premium learning time in disguise.

Make the last few minutes of your lesson free play. Let your child choose whatever game or activity they want.

Your child will prefer some parts of the lesson to others. Maybe they love moving their arms but hate practicing kicking. Maybe they love to glide but hate to float. It's easy to take the path of least resistance and avoid practicing the harder things, but it's important to practice them.

Make it more appealing by bookending the skills they don't like with ones your child enjoys most. The end-of-lesson playtime is a great reward for doing the things they'd rather not do during the rest of the lesson.

Enjoy this time yourself. Teaching is tiring work that requires you to be intensely focused on your child. Take a few deep breaths, soak in some rays, and share some laughs and hugs. The payoff you both experience during the end of the lesson will add to the eagerness you both feel to get back into the pool for your next lesson.

Being attuned to your child

It's easy to get caught up in your own plan for the lesson, but you and your child will do better if you focus on observing and responding to your child. The lesson plan is just a starting point. The more your child drives the lesson, the more tailored it will be to exactly what they need to learn and where they are developmentally.

Watch your child to see not only how they're doing with the skills but also how they're feeling. If they look nervous or afraid, move closer, provide more physical support, and heap on the praise for the effort they're making. If they look frustrated, take a break, backtrack to a skill you've already covered, or take a different approach to the skill you're practicing. You know your child. When they're frustrated, they might want more guidance, or they might want more space to try things independently.

When in doubt, help. If you're not sure whether your child needs more support, give it to them. It's important to make sure your child feels confident and secure. Fear and frustration make learning hard.

If something happens that scares your child—going underwater or breathing in water unexpectedly—acknowledge it. Be matter-of-fact about it. Make sure your own body language is confident and supportive. In the first few moments after an accident, your child looks to you to help them decide how to react and how to feel about it. How you respond helps your child make that decision.

Be sure to empathize with your child's feelings. Acknowledge not only that it happened but also that it was scary, if that's what your child tells you they feels Address how you'll keep it from happening again. Then move on.

It's a lot like dealing with boo-boos on dry land. "Did you fall? Does your knee hurt? I'm sorry. Do you need a bandage? How about a kiss? Next time, let's make sure to hold on with at least one hand when you're climbing. You ready to go again?" If you don't make a big deal out of it, your child will be less likely to.

If they look bored and they're not physically challenged by what you're practicing, congratulations! You've gone as far as you can with that skill for the lesson. Expand or refine the skill slightly to make it challenging again or move on to the next skill. If they look bored and they're still not quite getting it, switch to a game that uses the skill they're practicing instead of straight practice.

Try to spot early signs of cold or fatigue. If your child looks cold or physically uncomfortable, it's time to get out of the pool, dry off, sip a hot drink, and have a snack. As they get tired, their form will become sloppy, and that sloppy form is what your child will start to internalize and make into a habit. When you see your child's form—at whatever level of development it is—start to deteriorate during a lesson, call it quits.

Making the most of your time in the water

Once you're in the water, the clock is ticking. You have a limited amount of time before your child gets tired, hungry, cold, or burned out. Make the most of your time *in* the water by doing whatever you can to prepare when you're *out* of the water. Don't spend your valuable time in the water doing things you could do just as well on land.

Write your lesson plan on an index card and put it into a waterproof plastic bag. Read your lesson plan before you get into the water and refer to it during the lesson if you need to.

When you're practicing, have your child swim toward the wall or steps. Not only does it give your child something to aim for, but it's also a good habit to build so that they'll automatically head in that direction if they panic or needs to get out of the pool.

Bringing the lessons out of the pool

You have a major advantage over other swimming teachers when it comes to teaching your own child. You've got access to them when you're not in the pool. Although there's no way to learn to swim without getting in the water, there are lots of ways that you can enhance the learning process on dry land.

Observe

Kids learn by watching a good example. Have your child watch lap swimmers, and point out what's going on. "See how they turn their head to the side when they take a breath?"

Kids learn by watching other kids. Kids often learn to use swings by themselves within days after they watch other kids pumping their legs. Have your child watch other kids swim.

Ask a friend to record a video of your child while they swim so that you can watch it together later. The post-game analysis of their lesson lets your child see what's going right and wrong in a situation when they're not under pressure to remain afloat. It's a perfect way to use modern technology the way pro athletes have for a long time.

Have your child practice skills on land in front of the mirror. Your child can use you as a model and correct their body position based on what they see. You can highlight what's going on. "See how your head is tilted down now? How does it feel if you look up a bit? That's it." Suggest changes. Point out what's working.

Ask your child for their analysis of what's going on while they watch. How does a movement work? What parts of the body are involved? How does it feel? Does timing make a difference? Where are the parts of the body in relationship to each other and to the water?

Move

You can practice lots of movements on dry land, giving your child the opportunity to focus just on their body and to separate their movement from the need to keep their head above water. They can sit on the edge of a chair to practice kicks and flexing and pointing their toes. They can practice lying on their stomach and rolling side to side to get a sense for the motion of their torso in the water. They can stand up to practice body positions and arm movements.

The feelings will be different than they are in the water, but the benefit of having the completely secure feeling of being on land will let your child experience the feelings in their body thoroughly and without time pressure. They can take the insights they gain this way into the water with them.

Relax

You can practice relaxation techniques on dry land. Learning to swim will be easier if your child is relaxed. Kids tend to tense up under the pressure of learning a new skill in the water. You can help your child relax by teaching them how outside the water.

- Have them lie flat on their back.

- Ask them to make their body tight all over. You can help them by touching their body if they're having trouble. For example, you can touch their thigh and say, "squeeze this part of your body tight." You can ask them to squeeze one body part at a time, working their way up from their toes to their face.

- Have them hold their breath for a few seconds.

- Tell them to let it all go at once, and teach them a word for this. It could just be, "Relax," but a funny, made-up word that's your secret is more fun.

- After they relax their muscles, have them take a few deep belly breaths.

After you practice this relaxation technique regularly for a while on solid ground, you can transfer it to the pool. When you feel your child tensing up, say your secret, funny, made-up word for relax, and they'll know how to release the tension from their muscles.

Visualize

Studies have shown that athletes get as much benefit from visualizing their performance in great detail as they do from physically practicing (up to a point—you've got to get in the water, too). Many elite athletes use visualization as part of their training. It's safe. It's portable. It helps build confidence and comfort. It doesn't tire out your child's body. It's also a great distraction when you're stuck in traffic or waiting in line. (Just make sure the driver isn't doing the visualizing.)

Guide your child through a visualization of the skill you're working on. Paint them a picture with words. Use descriptions of what they'll be experiencing with all of their senses. Describe how the pool and the water look. Describe how the water feels. Describe the smell and the sounds of the pool. Describe how they'll move their body and how that will feel.

Putting it all together

You don't have to be perfect at this to have a great time with your child while you're teaching them to swim. Like any skill, teaching will get easier the more you do it. Remember to keep your goals in mind:

- Teaching your child to be water safe

- Making it a fun and intuitive experience

Remember to be patient with yourself and your child. Remember to refer to this book for tips and guidance if you need help. Trust yourself. You can do it.

Chapter 8
What to Do: 49 Tricks to Make Lessons Fun and Effective

Do create an atmosphere that's conducive to learning

- Do trust yourself.//
- Do relax.
- Do be patient with yourself.
- Do be patient with your child.
- Do use a nurturing, positive attitude.

- Do be calm but enthusiastic.

- Do be honest.

- Do think of the unspoken message your actions send your child.

Do make the most of time in the water

- Do start exposing your child to water as early in life as possible.

- Do have short, frequent lessons.

- Do provide as much opportunity to practice as possible, and make sure that a good chunk of that is unstructured.

- Do set aside time for a play activity that your child chooses in the middle and at the end of each lesson.

- Do teach in three to four feet of water, where an adult can stand firmly without feeling too buoyant.

- Do practice swimming toward the wall or steps.

Do fine-tune your teaching style

- Do tell your child what you'll be learning that day before you get into the pool.

- Do start easy and build on what your child has mastered.

- Do teach skills in small pieces that can be combined.

- Do teach one thing at a time.

- Do demonstrate.

- Do give simple, one- or two-word instructions.

- Do avoid yes/no questions.

- Do ask open-ended questions.

- Do repeat, practice, and review to turn movement into habit.

- Do acknowledge the small subtle things that are happening to your child's body.

- Do take time during the lesson to point out the physical sensations.

- Do praise your child's efforts, not just their accomplishments.

- Do be specific in your praise.

- Do give positive, specific, constructive, immediate feedback.

- Do define success based on process instead of outcome.

- Do encourage your child to try things they initiate (as long as you're there to keep them safe).

- Do use lots of different ways of explaining or showing.

- Do use all the senses to teach.

- Do touch the part of your child's body that you want them to focus on.

- Do use your hands to help adjust your child's body gently without forcing them.

- Do relate the thing you're trying to teach to something your child already knows how to do, like dig a hole or pedal a bike.

- Do use imagination, games, and visualization to make repetition and practice fun.

Do be attuned to your child's needs

- Do check in frequently to see how your child feels.

- Do help your child reframe nervousness as excitement.

- Do watch your child and respond to their needs.

- Do observe your child for signs of fatigue or cold.

- Do stop if your child gets tired or cold.

- Do acknowledge it, empathize, and move on, if something scary—like swallowing water—happens.

- Do switch to a different approach or to a different skill if your child gets frustrated.

- Do be aware of when your child needs you to give more support or back off and let them try things independently.

- Do help, if you're not sure whether your child needs help.

Chapter 9
What Not to Do: Fifteen Sure-fire Ways to Keep Your Lesson Afloat

Don't lose your child's trust

- Don't throw your child into the water to teach them to swim, ever.
- Don't force your child into water without preparing them.
- Don't deny it if your child has a scary moment.
- Don't trick your child or lie.

Don't send your child subtle messages that they should fear the water

- Don't wipe it off if water gets on your face or your child's face.
- Don't prevent them from trying new things in the water.
- Don't overreact if they swallow some water.
- Don't yell.

Don't let your expectations interfere with your child's progress

- Don't expect your child's swimming to be fast, especially in the beginning.
- Don't expect very young kids to learn strokes before they're developmentally ready.
- Don't expect your child to pick up right away where you left off at the end of the last lesson.
- Don't expect your child to do it perfectly.

Chapter 10
What Your Child Needs to Learn

Your goal is to help your child learn to be water safe. They need to know how to move their body in the water, to take a breath while their body is in the water, and to get from the water to dry land. Even when your child is water safe, there's still risk associated with swimming, as there is with anything else in life.

Good indicators that your child has enough skill to be safe in the water are:

- They can swim the width or length of the pool, easily taking breaths as necessary.

- They can tread water for at least three minutes in any depth.

- They can get into the pool by themselves easily, either by jumping in from the side or from a seated position on the edge of the pool.

- They can get out of the pool by themselves easily, by grabbing the side of the pool and pulling themselves out or by swimming to the stairs or ladder and climbing out.

- They can pick things up from the bottom of the pool.

Teaching them the following skills will give them the foundation they need to be water safe. This chapter gives you the fundamental sequence of skills and straightforward steps for teaching them.

Remember to tailor the teaching to the way your child learns. Look to Chapter 11 for ideas about how to add imagination and play to the learning process for each skill.

Sequence of skills

When you're teaching, you need to start with the simple and work toward the complex. You need to start with the easy and build toward the difficult.

Each of the following skills provides a basis for the skills that follow it. Working through the skills in this order will allow your child to feel confident and achieve competence at each stage of the learning process.

- Getting into the pool

- Feeling the water

- Holding onto the wall and climbing out

- Blowing bubbles

- Putting their head under water

- Kicking

- Gliding in streamline or torpedo position
- Popup breathing
- Body shape and position
- Treading water
- Moving underwater
- Back float
- Rudimentary crawl and backstroke
- Turning their head to breathe

Getting into the pool

The younger your child is when you start teaching them to swim, the better. Although kids may not be coordinated enough to master the strokes until they're four or five, they can become comfortable with the water much earlier. That comfort will make learning to swim much easier.

Kids without experience in the water tend to develop a fear of the water as they get older. Most three- and four-year-olds don't have an entrenched fear of the water. Seven- and eight-year-olds without swimming experience often do.

This fear is reasonable. Being careful around the water is always smart, but before you've learned to swim, that caution comes from a constant awareness of the possibility of drowning. Kids learn about that possibility in a variety of ways. They remember slips in the bathtub. They swallow water the wrong way and cough when they're learning to drink out of a cup. They see characters in cartoons struggling before going under permanently. They listen to older kids.

Your goal for teaching your child to get into the pool is for them to be able to get into the pool safely by themselves. They'll do this either by using the stairs or pool ladder, by sitting on the edge of the pool and lowering themselves in, or by standing on the edge and jumping into the pool, assuming it's at least five feet deep.

Initially, though, you'll be providing lots of physical and emotional support. As your child becomes more comfortable, you'll gradually remove that support and give them more independence.

The first stage

Start by getting into the water with your child. You should work on this in water that's shallow enough for you to feel securely balanced and not too buoyant when you stand, around three to four feet deep.

Have your child sit on the edge of the pool. Sit next to them. Keeping one hand on your child to make sure they're secure, lower yourself into the water.

Turn to face them, move your body close to the edge of the pool so that your body is just touching their legs, and grasp their waist firmly but gently with your hands. Reassure them that you have a firm grip. Lift them and hold them against your body.

Initially, having lots of body contact will help your child feel secure. They'll feel most secure if their whole body is touching yours. Eye contact will also help your child feel secure. Hold your child close to your body.

Practice the first stages of feeling the water and holding onto the wall and getting out before moving on to the next stage.

Dealing with fear of the water

If your child is afraid of the water, your best tool is patience. You might already know where their fear originated or how it developed. If you don't, probe gently for an answer. It's possible that their fear stems from a misconception that you can quickly correct.

If your child becomes upset or doesn't want to talk about their fear, don't force them. Instead, start very slowly to work on getting them comfortable with the water *before* trying to get into the water.

Point out other kids playing in the water and let your child watch without pressuring them to get in. Point out the ways that water is already a part of their life—from drinking, to taking a bath, to playing in the rain or running through the sprinklers.

Have your child sit near the pool. Get your hands wet and gently stroke your child with your wet hands, spreading the water first on their arms and legs and then on their hair and face.

See if they'll dip their fingers into the water with you next to them. Encourage them to dip just their feet, and then their legs, into the water while you stand in the pool in front of them.

Don't force your child into the water. If they start to become upset with something you're trying, stop and go back to an activity they're comfortable with, even if it's just taking a sip of water. Be supportive and patient, and work to keep your own expectations under control. If your child is still as afraid as ever after a few weeks of gently easing them into contact with the water, consider taking a break from trying for a while. If they remain very afraid after weeks of trying and a break, consider having them work through the fear with a child psychologist.

If your child is too afraid of the water to take a bath, they're not ready to learn to swim. Try having them sit in an empty tub and play with toys while you sit with them, either in the tub or just outside the tub.

When they become comfortable with that, offer them a warm glass of water or a bucket that they can pour into the tub themselves when they feel like it. Over the course of several weeks, go through the exercise every day, gradually moving to adding increasing amounts of water from the faucet. Only after your child is completely comfortable in the bath should you consider trying to start to teach them to swim.

The next stage

Step 1
As your child gains confidence in the water and with the feel of the water, a lighter touch will work.

Again, have your child sit on the edge of the pool. Sit next to them. Keeping one hand on your child to make sure they're secure, lower yourself into the water.

Turn to face them but instead of moving so that your body is touching them, reach your arms out to pick them up and bring them to you. Hold them so that less of their body is touching yours.

Step 2
Start using their imaginative and problem-solving skills to explore this skill. Ask them questions. How many different ways are there to get into the pool? Are some of them safer than others? Why? Which are the best ways?

If some of their ideas aren't safe, point out why. Try their other ideas with them.

And, finally

Step 1
Once your child feels very comfortable in the water, they're ready to get into the pool feet-first all by themselves. Ease into having them move themselves from a seated position on the edge of the pool into your waiting arms. Start by standing close enough that they can reach out and touch you, but make sure they're the one reaching for you, not the other way around.

Step 2
Gradually move back so that you're standing a foot or more from the edge of the pool and your child has to lean forward and scoot into the pool to reach you. Once they're able to stabilize themselves in the pool

by holding onto the edge, have them lower themselves into the water and hold onto the edge while you're standing nearby.

Feeling the water

The one thing that will contribute the most to your child's learning to swim is their development of a feel for the water. Awareness of how their body feels in the water and reacts to the water and how the water reacts to their body is the foundation of every skill your child needs to learn in order to be water safe.

In the water, your child's balance will be different than it is on land. Instead of feeling their center of gravity, they'll feel a center of buoyancy. Instead of feeling a sense of easy movement through space, they'll feel a sense of resistance. Instead of pushing forward to move forward, they'll push backwards to move forward. Explicitly exploring and developing awareness of all of these differences will help your child learn each skill more quickly and effectively.

The first stage

Before you even get into the pool, you and your child can play with your hands in the water to get a sensual feel for how the body and water move together. You can do this in the bathtub or even using a big pot of water on the kitchen table.

Push against the water with your palm. Then slice through it with the side of your hand like a karate chop. Feel the difference. Expand your exploration of movement through the water to larger parts of the body—the arm, the leg. (You're probably going to need the tub for the larger parts of the body, unless you've got really big pots in your kitchen.)

Try pushing and pulling through the water with fingers spread apart and again with fingers tightly together. Use a cupped palm and a flat palm. Discuss how these movements feel. Discuss their effect on the water. Which movements are harder and which are easier? Which move the water more? Which make bigger splashes?

The next stage

Step 1
While you hold your child, lower your body into the water or move into deeper water, where you can still stand comfortably, so that the water is up to your shoulders. Make sure that you keep your child's face level with your own to keep from accidentally getting water into their nose or mouth. Walk around in the water so that your child feels the flow of water around their body.

Step 2
Experiment with different ways of moving your arms and legs through the water. Make big splashes. Make little splashes. You can do this while you're holding them or while they sit on the steps.

Step 3
Once your child is confident in the water while you're holding them close, create a bit of distance between your bodies and practice what you've already learned that way.

Step 4
Play with bouncing in the water so that your child starts to develop a sense of their own buoyancy and balance in the water.

Step 5
You can progressively move your bodies farther apart until you're holding your child just under the arms or by the hands.

And, finally

At each stage of the learning process and for each skill you learn, devote some time specifically to feeling the water and its interaction with the body.

When they've learned to put their head underwater, to do the streamline position, and to kick, have your child experiment and explore.

Step 1

What happens if you push off from the side with your arms or legs? What happens if you move your arms backwards? Forwards? Up or down? This experimentation is critical, because these things are all different than they are on dry land. Moving your arms backwards propels you forward in the water. Moving your arms down propels you up. Starting to understand this will give your child confidence and control in the water.

Step 2

Have your child solve problems. How can you go backwards in the water? How can you go forward? Which movements and positions move you with the least effort? Which movements and positions move you with the least splash? Help your child learn to push back to go forward and down to go up.

Step 3

Practice moving through the water like a fish or a ninja, disturbing the water as little as possible. How big a splash can you make for fun? How do you do it? Practice sitting on the steps and hitting the water with the flat, broad parts of your body. Okay, now how small a splash can you make? Can you slice your hand into the water without seeing any ripples at all? Practice no-ripple swimming. You're learning to sneak up on Mom or Dad in the water, so that you can pounce on them.

Kids will discover these things on their own by playing in the water, but you can speed up the process by specifically guiding your child.

Holding onto the wall and climbing out

Your child needs to know how to get out of the pool safely. Even when they're not yet a strong swimmer, this one skill can help to save your child's life.

The first stage

While you hold your child by the waist, have them hold onto the edge with both hands. Keep a firm grip, but reduce the amount of support you're providing so that your child's body is supported by the water. Have them practice moving along the wall by pulling themselves with their hands.

The next stage

Stand next to your child while they hold onto the edge of the pool with both hands. Keep a gentle touch on their back so that they know that you're there if they need you. Move with them as they pull themselves with their hands to the ladder or stairs. Hold their waist or support their back as they climb out.

And, finally

Stand back from your child while they hold onto the wall and move themselves. Stay near them but out of reach, and let them climb the ladder or stairs to get out of the pool by themselves.

Blowing bubbles

You won't see a 200-meter bubble-blowing event in the next Olympics. Nonetheless, learning to blow bubbles is an important skill. It's a stepping stone to learning breath control, which your child will use whenever they're in the water for the rest of their life.

Blowing bubbles teaches your child to be comfortable putting and keeping their face in the water. It teaches them to take deep breaths in and to control letting their breath out. It encourages them to play with holding their breath. All of these things are integral elements of breathing while swimming.

The first stage

Step 1
You can practice blowing bubbles without getting into the water. Blow on your child's hand. Have them blow on their own hand. This practice will help them to get the feel of blowing. So will blowing bubbles with soapy water and a bubble wand. You can also practice with balloons. Always supervise young children with balloons, because balloons are a choking hazard.

Step 2
You can practice blowing bubbles through a straw into water in a glass. Then, you can practice blowing bubbles directly in the water, in the tub or in a large bowl or pot of water. Remember to supervise your child even when you're using these small amounts of water.

Tip 1
If your child is nervous about putting their face in the water, dip your hand into the water and stroke their face with your wet hand. Then encourage them to put just their lips into a saucer of water. Move from there to slightly more water in a bowl. From there, you can encourage them to put their lips into the water in a bathtub.

Tip 2
The intake of breath that you need to start blowing bubbles is a step toward holding your breath. Blowing into a young child's face causes them to hold their breath for a moment. This can also help you teach your child the feeling of holding their breath.

The next stage

Step 1
After your child can blow bubbles in water in a tub, have them practice blowing bubbles in the pool while you hold them. Have them try to take in and spit out water.

Step 2

Practice having them hold their breath out of the water. Demonstrate by taking an exaggerated breath in, puffing up your cheeks, and holding your nose. Have them do the same. Have them try it again without holding their nose. At first, they can hold their finger right under their nose to make sure no air is being taken in or leaking out through their nose.

Step 3

When they can hold their breath out of the water for several seconds, have them practice holding their breath and putting their whole face in the water for just a moment. You can practice this in a bowl of water or in the bathtub first.

Important note!

Don't force their head, and don't rest your hand on the back of their head while their face is under the water. Doing either of those things will make your child feel a loss of control that will make it hard for you to convince them to try again.

Step 4

When they're comfortable with putting their face in the water, have them hold their breath and put their face in the water for several seconds. You can have them count to three in their head, or you can tap on their back once a second, telling them to lift their head whenever they need to but to try to hold their breath until you tap their back three times. If you spot a burst of bubbles coming out of the water, it means they've lost the hang of it and you should lift their head out of the water for the moment.

Step 5

Practice what you've tried in the tub in the pool. Hold their body close to yours so that they feel supported.

And, finally

Have your child practice holding their breath with their face in the water until they can hold their breath for ten seconds or so. Have them practice repeating the process of holding their breath with their face in the water, lifting their face to take another breath, and putting their face back in the water. Once they can do this, they have the skills they need to put their head under the water.

Putting their head underwater

Once your child knows how to hold their breath and put their face in the water, it's still a jump to put their whole head under the water. The pressure they'll feel in their nose and ears will be uncomfortable and unfamiliar, and it will take a lot of practice to make dunking their whole head feel effortless and unremarkable.

The first stage

Step 1

Demonstrate what you're aiming for. Watching you do each step will help your child see what's possible and understand what they'll be doing.

Step 2

While you hold your child, have them hold their breath and put the side of their face in the water. Have them gently lower their cheek into the water so that it's fully submerged but their nose isn't in the water. This will give them their first experience of having water fill their ear. Try it on both sides.

The next stage

Step 1

Once they're used to putting their cheeks in the water, practice moving their body while they're in this position. You can hold them so that they're lying on their side in the water or cradled on their side in your arms, whichever feels more comfortable for them. Have them face you so that they can look up to make eye contact if they need the extra security.

Step 2
Start moving your child's body gently, always moving in the direction of the top of their head. This will allow the water to flow over their face toward their chin and will keep water from getting into their nose.

Step 3
Have your child put their whole head in the water by themselves while you hold them. It's easiest if they put their head in the water face first. Have them start with their mouth in the water first, then the rest of their face, and finally the rest of their head.

This way of entering the water is less likely to force water up their nose. Let them hold their nose if that's a concern.

Tip
Encourage your child to burp. Learning to hold your breath often involves swallowing some air.

And, finally

Step 1
Practice going underwater together, holding your child securely against your body.

Explain what you'll be doing. If your child expresses fear, don't do it. Work towards it instead. Keep practicing putting their head in the water face first.

Count to three. Rise up a little with a fairly quick, sharp movement, make a big show of taking a loud deep breath, complete with puffed out cheeks. For a lot of kids, the quick, sharp lift triggers an intake of breath. Quickly and smoothly lower both of you under water for just a second, maintaining eye contact the whole time, even under water.

Tip

If you move slightly sideways into the water as you go under, water is less likely to get into your child's nose. You can try having your child hold their nose with their fingers the first few times if they're worried about their nose. Once they gain confidence, do it without holding the nose.

Tip

If your child sputters, demonstrate a little cough to clear your own throat. Praise and explain that it will get easier.

Step 2

Keep practicing and repeating this exercise, gradually extending the time under water to a few seconds. When they feel really comfortable, go underwater together having them hold onto you by your arms, so that there's plenty of space between your bodies and they have a strong feeling of independence in the movement.

Step 3

As a last step toward mastering putting their head underwater, have your child hold onto the edge of the pool with you nearby but not touching them. Have them put their own head under the water, preparing themselves and choosing for themselves when to resurface.

Tip

If that's too challenging, put your own hand on the edge of the pool and start by having your child hold the edge of the pool with one hand and your hand—the one that's holding the edge of the pool—with their other hand.

Kicking

In most strokes, kicking provides stability for your body while the arms provide most of the propulsion. The kick helps your body to stay aligned. In the early learning stages, having a solid flutter kick will help stabilize your child as they learn to position their body in the water and to use their arms to propel themselves.

The key to the kick is coordination and ankle flexibility. Six aspects of the kick to focus on are:

- There should be a lot of movement in the ankle, but from the hip to the ankle should be supple but almost straight. The knees should bend very little. It's not like pedaling a bike. Think length and flow.

- Use the muscles at the top of the thigh to move the whole leg.

- The leg shouldn't have side-to-side movement.

- The kick should be narrow, with ankles fairly close to each other.

- The kick isn't long like a stride on land is. The up-down movement should be contained within the movement of the water that your arms creates. You can feel this area when you move your body. When you get to the part of the water that hasn't been moved by your body, your leg will feel more resistance. Keep your kick out of that higher-resistance water.

- Ankle flexibility is really important. While your whole leg moves, the foot is like a flipper that provides most of the benefit of the movement. It should feel like you're trying to flick a shoe off your foot.

The first stage

Step 1
Start by practicing on dry land. Have your child sit in a chair. Demonstrate what it means to flex and to point, and have them practice it without any kicking motion. Have them hold still while you move their feet for them from flexed to pointed and back again, so that they really feel the ankle and can isolate that feeling.

Step 2
Have your child sit on the edge of the chair and brace themselves with their hands. Ask them to lean their torso back slightly for balance and

kick from the hip, keeping their legs straight, their ankles loose, and the kick small and narrow. Use this opportunity to touch their upper thigh to show them where the work is being done.

They won't get a great sense from this exercise for how important the ankles are, because air resistance is so much less than water resistance, but they will get a good feel for keeping their legs straight and for the range of motion from the hip.

Tip

Don't introduce all of the ideas at once. Start with focusing on straight legs. Once your child has the idea, switch the focus to the ankles and think only about ankles for a while. Add a new layer of information only when your child feels comfortable with what they've already learned.

The next stage

Tip

Fins can help kids without much buoyancy to keep their legs and hips in line with their torsos as they learn to use their arms in the water; however, long-term, they'll become a crutch, and they'll alter the quality and feeling of the movement in a way that doesn't help when your child is learning to kick.

You can use fins during the early stages of learning to swim when your child is focusing on other skills, but don't use fins when your child is practicing kicking.

Step 1

Practicing the kick at the stairs is a good place to start because it lets your child hold their body even with the surface easily. If they're not using the stairs to support themselves, support them with one arm under their belly and the other hand holding their hands.

Have them hold their face in the water, and ask them to squeeze your hand whenever they want to come up for a breath. When they do, they can press down on their hands to help themselves lift their head. You can help them by holding the hand that's holding theirs firm.

Walk around the pool as they practice. Remind them to flick their feet like they're trying to kick off their shoes.

And, finally

Step 1
When your child has gotten experience floating on their back—and we work on that much later for good reason—you can come back to kicking and expand their practice of their kick. Have them practice gently kicking while they're floating on their back.

Tip
If they move in the direction of their feet, it's a sign that their ankles aren't flexing enough. Have them concentrate on flexing their ankles more, and like magic, they'll start to move toward their head. This level of flexion is what they're aiming for.

Step 2
When they've learned to move their arms in the crawl and backstroke, they can refine their kick more. There's a rhythm to kicking: kick, kick, pause, kick, kick, pause. The opposite leg and arm act together. In that way, it's similar to running or walking. When they stroke with the left arm, they should kick with the right leg first.

Gliding in streamline or torpedo position

When your child can put they head under the water and kick, they're ready to learn the streamline or torpedo position. This position will help your child learn to keep their body in a position that minimizes the amount of drag their body creates and helps them to move through the water with less resistance.

The first stage

Step 1
You can practice the torpedo position on dry land. Have your child lie on their back and look straight up at the ceiling. Ask them to extend their arms overhead so that their whole body is flat on the ground and their body is a straight line from the tips of their fingers to the tips of their toes.

Have your child place the thumb of one hand where the thumb and first finger of the other hand meet. Then, have them rotate their hands slightly so that the fingers overlap. The shape of the hands is like a triangle, with the overlapped fingers forming a point.

Their head should be in line with their arms, not tucked down or tilted back. When they're lying on the ground looking straight up at the ceiling, this will be the position their head naturally assumes.

Tip
In the water, kids have a tendency to lift the head up and keep it out of the water. A guideline that helps the head position is to make sure your ears are touching your upper arms. Ask your child to squeeze their ears with their arms to feel their position.

Step 2
Have them practice the same position standing straight up and looking straight forward. Keeping their body in this position without the guidance of the floor is only slightly harder.

The next stage

Step 1
In the pool, have your child get into streamline position and then put their face into the water. Help them glide through the water by facing them, holding both of their hands, and walking backwards.

Step 2

Getting started moving is the hardest part. When your child is comfortable with having you tow them while they're in streamline position, have them push off from the step or the side and glide into your arms. Gradually increase the distance of the glide.

You can also do this back and forth with two people. It's like playing catch with a person as the ball.

Tip

Even when your child starts doing glides by themselves, stay close, both for their safety and to make them feel secure and confident. Don't have them try incorporating the kick yet.

And, finally

When your child is completely comfortable with gliding in streamline position, have them child push off from the edge in streamline position and begin to kick. Have them practice until they can move the width of the pool this way.

Popup breathing

Until your child starts working on keeping their head in the water and turning it slightly to the side to take a breath, they'll lift their whole head out of the water when they need to breathe. In order to do this, they'll need to understand that to lift up out of the water they'll push down with their arms.

The first stage

Step 1

Have your child sit on the steps so that the water is up to the tops of their shoulders. If this won't work with the steps of your pool, hold your child gently around the waist and lower both of you so that the water reaches the tops of their shoulders.

Have them extend their arms in front of them and press down, cupping their hands. They should feel their body rise up while they're pushing down and sink back down when they're finished. Have them try doing it with their arms bent at different angles and with their fingers spread apart instead of closed.

Step 2

Talk about it. Discuss with them how the different ways they move their arms and hands affect how their body moves. Does pushing harder make a difference? What does pushing down do? What does pushing up do? What difference does each variation of the movement make?

Step 3

Have your child practice pushing down with their arms, bringing their arms close to their body and lifting them up like arrows through the water, and pushing them down again.

Discuss how making their arms like arrows going straight up through the water feels compared to the pushing down they've been practicing. They should notice that it's easier to move their arms through the water when they're slicing through it like an arrow, and that their body barely moves when they use their arms this way.

Step 4

Have them practice this sequence repeatedly, so that they're maximizing resistance while they push down and minimizing resistance while they bring their arms back to the surface.

Have them push down, bring their arms to the surface, push down, and bring their arms to the surface several times without stopping. Discuss how that keeps their body lifted in the water.

The next stage

Step 1

Explain what you'll be doing before you start. While you're supporting their body with an arm under their stomach, have your child glide in torpedo position from one side of the pool to the other. Halfway across the pool, have them push down with their arms and lift their head to take a breath. Hold them as firmly as necessary while they try it.

Work your way to having them try to pop up for a breath halfway across the pool while your arms are just grazing their belly, providing no real physical support. Then walk beside they while they take a popup breath on their own.

And, finally

Have your child practice pushing off from the side and swimming across the pool to you, stopping to pop up for a breath whenever they need one.

Body shape and position

When fish swim, they're graceful. They're balanced. They're slippery. They move efficiently, with each motion propelling them through the water.

A well designed boat slices through the water, creating as little resistance and drag as possible.

The shape and position of the body in the water make a huge difference to how well the body moves through the water. Before even considering teaching your child strokes, you have to teach them to feel their body in the water and to shape their body in the water.

The first stage

You're aiming for a long, balanced body position. The longer you can make your body in the water, the faster you'll move. Kids tend to revert to a dog paddling position, with their bodies close to vertical in the water and their arms bent and close to their bodies.

Step 1

Have your child lie on the ground outside the pool or at home, on their back or their stomach. Don't forget to put a towel down to make them comfortable if you're practicing on hard ground. Ask them how their body feels while they're lying down. What's the feeling in their limbs? How about in their belly? What about their head? Compare this to how it feels to sit or stand.

Step 2

Practice the streamlined position until it feels natural. Have your child practice not just lifting their arms overhead but stretching them as if they're reaching for something just beyond their fingertips. Keep the body in a streamline position, with the arms reaching forward, the arms and head in line with the torso, the chest pressing down into the water, and the legs in line with the torso. Practice it on the ground outside the pool.

The next stage

Step 1

In the pool, you can practice doing streamline glides on the stomach, back, and sides to get a feel for the differences.

Step 2

Have your child concentrate on the difference between how their body moves in the water when they're dog paddling and how it moves when they're streamlined.

Step 3

Ask your child to try things in the water. How would your body move if you were really slippery? What could you do to feel slippery in the water? How would your body move if it weighed nothing? What could you do to feel like you weigh nothing in the water? (Practice shifting balance to see what feels more like weightlessness.)

And, finally

Eventually, most of your child's time swimming will be spent rolling from side to side, slicing through the water, instead of on their stomach, pushing through the water. Because of the way the shoulder joint moves, swimming on your side allows you to be even longer. You can give your child a feel for this on land. Have them stand facing a wall with their body touching it. Ask them to stretch both hands up. Have them keep their fingertips against the wall and twist their torso from side to side.

When the side of their body twists close to the wall, that arm reaches higher than it does when their torso is flat against the wall. The same thing happens in the water. Doing this will also help them feel how their core and back muscles move when they rotate. Eventually, that's what your child will aim for in the water.

Treading water

Treading water is important for water safety. While many swimming programs emphasize floating, floating is actually a more advanced skill. Although floating helps kids to learn the idea of how their body should be positioned in the water—horizontally—their body composition and shape make it very tough for kids to learn to float without moving.

Treading water, on the other hand, is an easy, natural motion for your child. It will give them confidence in the water and help to develop their feel for how their body moves in the water.

The first stage

Stand next to your child in the water, supporting them. Ask them to dig holes with their hands and ride a bike with their legs. Gradually reduce the amount of support you're providing, but let them grab you for support or a break whenever they need to.

The next stage

Make sure your child's chin is up, pointing at the sky. Make sure their arms and legs stay under the water instead of thrashing in the air. Have them practice until they feel confident treading water while you're a pace or two out of their reach.

And, finally

Step 1

When they're first learning to tread water, your child will get tired easily. They'll move their arms and legs quickly. It's counterintuitive, but moving their arms and legs slowly will support them better than moving them quickly. Have them experiment with speed.

Step 2

As they become more comfortable, have them experiment with moving their legs like old-fashioned eggbeaters. With both of their legs bent at the hip and the knee, as if they're sitting in a chair, have your child move first one leg and then the other, with the motion coming from the knee. Ask them to draw a big circle in the water with one toe and then the other, moving the toe forward and then toward the center of their body before bringing it back, away from the center, and forward again.

Step 3

Have them work toward moving both legs at the same time. The rhythmic, alternating movement of the legs means that when one foot is forward, the other foot is back. This method of moving the legs is so efficient that it allows you to tread water without using the arms at all.

Step 4

Have them practice making figure 8's with their hands, making their hands into cups to maximize water resistance.

Step 5

Have your child practice treading water with as little effort as possible. If they're breathing hard, ask them to slow down. Take as many breaks as necessary, support as much of your child's weight as necessary to make them feel comfortable, and work toward the point where your child can tread water for five minutes without taking a break, touching the bottom, or holding onto you or the side of the pool.

Moving underwater

Once they have a feel for moving in the water and for breath control, most kids love to dive under the water. It's fun and freeform and as close to being a fish as you can get.

The first stage

Have your child stand in the pool in a spot where they can touch the bottom. Ask them to touch their toes. Next, drop sinking toys or coins and have them pick them up.

The next stage

Step 1
Move to deeper water. Have your child hold onto the edge of the pool and try to pick up sinking toys or coins from the bottom.

Step 2
Show them how to move their hands from their thighs into a palms-together position and then move them like an arrow into streamline position.

Next, have them turn their hands so that their palms face away from each other, shape their palms into cups, and pull their arms outward, away from the midline of the body, until their hands touch their thighs. Elbows should be slightly bent. Have them practice this motion out of the water and on the surface.

Step 3

Have your child practice using the movement from Step 2 to propel them to the bottom of the pool. At this stage, they can use a flutter kick for adding propulsion and control.

Step 4

Once they feel comfortable with their arm motions, have them try moving their legs like a frog to kick. They should bring their heels to their bottom and then kick both feet out to the sides with their ankles flexed.

When their feet are extended to the sides, they can flick their feet like flippers to point their feet and bring the soles of their feet together, legs straight. Have them practice the movement while they're lying on their stomach on dry land.

Tip

The power of this kick comes from the flick of the ankles and the quickness of the return to straight legs.

And, finally

Have them play with the movements. How would a fish move through the water? How about a frog? A dolphin? A whale? A shark?

Have them swim under water from one side of the pool to pick up a sinking toy or coin you've dropped on the bottom of the other side.

Back float

People tend to think of floating as basic, but it takes a lot of practice. Even for adults, floating without moving is tough. Floating is about getting a feel for buoyancy and your body. For kids, who are less buoyant, it can be one of the hardest things to master. It can feel precarious for kids without much body fat. We're most buoyant in the lungs, but even if the chest remains near the surface, the legs and lower body will tend to sink. The sinking feeling can cause kids to panic.

The first stage

Step 1
The back float is an ideal skill to practice on dry land. Most kids don't like the feeling of being in the water on their backs. They tend to try to lift their heads and bend at the waist, which makes them sink. Practicing on land helps them to get a feel for what to expect of their bodies before they have to cope with the water. Have your child lie on their back on dry land and focus on keeping their shoulder blades and bottom touching the floor and their legs and arms relaxed. Have them tilt their head back so that their chin is pointing up.

Step 2
Use the bathtub to help your child get used to the sensation of lying on their back in the water with the water over their ears. Have them lie on their back while the pool fills or drains and the water is just deep enough to cover their ears. Lie in the bath yourself with your child lying on top of you on their back. They'll get used to the sensation of being buoyant and floating but feel completely supported by your body.

The next stage

Step 1
In the water, hold your child with their back to your chest, so that they feel strongly supported. Lower both of you into the water, keeping your child's head touching your body with their shoulders resting on your chest. Standing behind your child is useful, because their desire to see your face will help them to keep their head tilted back.

Tip
You can make your child more comfortable by using your shadow to cover their face while they're learning to float. They won't have to squint into a glare or turn to avoid it, and their tendency to try to see your face will help them to tilt their head back.

Tip
Often people tell kids to lift their bellies or hips when they're trying to float. Instead, try telling your child to press their chest down. Make sure they keeps their head in line with their body. Lifting their head will make them sink.

Lifting any body part out of the water makes floating difficult or impossible. Try it yourself. Float on your back and see what happens if you lift your arm. It throws off your balance and decreases your buoyancy.

Step 2
Have your child practice floating in the bathtub if they're small enough.

And, finally

As they feel comfortable, gradually move your body so that you're providing support only with your hands on their head. Don't remove support too fast. Your child's first reaction to feeling insecure will be to try to sit up, which makes floating impossible.

The part of the face that should be sticking out during floating is really small. The water should come almost to the outer corners of the eyes. Once they feel comfortable floating without moving their body too much, have them focus on the position of their head and face. Ask them to concentrate on feeling the water lapping against their cheeks and touching their forehead and the outside corners of their eyes.

Front crawl

The front crawl is the most efficient way to move your body on the surface of the water. It's a complex stroke. Adults work for years to become proficient at it. Entire books have been written on it. These steps will provide you and your child an introduction to learning the crawl.

The parts of the crawl to focus on are arm movement, leg movement, torso movement, breathing, and timing and synchronization of movement.

The first stage

By this point, your child has the advantage of having learned to put their head under water, to kick, to streamline their body position, and to breathe when they need to. All of this is the foundation for starting to learn the front crawl.

The work kicking in streamline position has prepared your child to keep their body horizontal and their head in line with the rest of their body. This is the necessary starting point for the crawl. If your child is still holding their body closer to vertical or mostly horizontal but with their head lifted up, keep practicing the streamline position until that's completely comfortable before you start to work on the crawl.

Step 1

To start to learn the crawl, ask your child to pull one of their arms from streamline position through the water to their thigh. Have them return that arm to streamline position and then try the same thing with their other arm. Have them practice alternating their arms this way until they feel comfortable with it. They should continue to pop up to breathe during this early practice.

Initially, your child will probably move their arm through the water to return it to streamline position. That's fine at this stage of learning.

Step 2

Have your child visualize reaching for something just beyond their grasp. Since kids tend to revert to dog paddle arms, with everything pulled close to their body, exaggerate the idea of keeping arms long for each stroke.

Later, using a bent elbow to allow the arm to spend as little time out of the water as possible will be important. Early on, though, overcorrecting away from the dog paddle is helpful.

Step 3

At first, your child might have to concentrate so hard on moving their arms that they forget to keep kicking. Don't worry about this. After they've gotten some experience moving their arms, gently remind them to kick. Work on this until your child is comfortable stroking with their arms and kicking continuously.

The next stage

Step 1

Ask your child to think about grabbing a handful of water and pulling it down to their hip. Have them imagine that they're trying to keep the water from falling out of their hand. They should keep their fingers together and their palm gently cupped. How does it feel?

Step 2

Have your child concentrate on pulling back with their hand, not pushing down on the water. Remember that pushing backwards helps you go forward and pushing down helps you go up. When your arm is in the water, pull it back, and don't push it down.

Any part of the motion that's downward is moving your child up in the water, which is not the direction they want to go. Not only is it not moving them forward, it's also increasing drag and slowing them down. Pushing sideways also moves them in the wrong direction. Focus on pulling back.

Once they're comfortable with this, let them practice it until kicking simultaneously comes naturally.

Step 3

During this stage of learning, your child will naturally start to play with the timing of their arm movements. Encourage them to do this. What happens if you start moving one arm back while the other arm is pulling back? What happens if you start moving one arm back while the other arm is returning to streamline position? Foster an awareness of timing and the different results different approaches to timing yield.

Step 4
At this stage, your child's arms will be stretched out straight throughout the stroke, both when they're pulling their arm backwards and when they're returning it to streamline position. During the part of the stroke when your arm is moving forward, you're not helping to propel yourself forward. (Remember push back to go forward.)

You have to get your arm ahead of you again, though. For the forward movement, there's less resistance moving your arm through the air than through the water. Have your child focus on lifting their arm out of the water to return to streamline position.

Eventually, they'll bend at the elbow to return their arm to the forward position as quickly as possible. At this stage, though, just keeping their arm out of the water is a big accomplishment.

Step 5
At this point, you can start working on turning their head to breathe, as explained later in this chapter, instead of doing popup breathing.

And, finally

Step 1
Ask your child to imagine having their body move through the smallest possible hole in the water. How small can they make the hole? Can they be like a spear or an arrow moving through the water? Can they be like a needle moving through the water? Can they be silent and move without a splash? What body positions can help them do this?

And all the steps beyond
The basics they've learned so far will put them in the top ten percent of understanding of all swimmers. If you'd like to help them learn more, you can focus on sophisticated refinements. Remember, though. Only add one thing to focus on at a time, and only after the more basic aspects of the skill have been mastered.

- Use leverage. When they pull their arm through the water, have your child bend at the elbow. A bent arm applies more force given the same amount of effort. Try this on land. Have your child pick up something with a bent arm and again with a straight arm. The bent arm makes it easier to move the same weight.

- Have your child bend their arm at the elbow during the recovery phase of the stroke, the part of the stroke when their arm is returning to streamline position. Have them aim to have their arm enter the water just above their ear, instead of extended straight in front of them.

- Have your child try slicing into the water with their hand, with the thumb entering the water first.

- Have your child try rolling onto their side as their hand enters the water. This rolling motion of the torso provides power. The sideways position of the water presents a smaller surface area to the water so that there's less resistance. The angle of the shoulder when their body is on its side allows for greater range of motion. This is complex. It takes many hours of practice to master.

- In addition to alternating with the arms, your child can practice alternating with their legs. When their right arm enters the water, have them try to kick first with their left leg.

- Have your child play with the timing of the rolling motion, of the arm recovery, of the movement of the arm into the water.

- Have your child experiment with the number of strokes they take between breaths.

- Have your child count the number of strokes it takes for them to swim the length of the pool. Can they focus on making each stroke better so that they can swim the length of the pool in fewer strokes?

Backstroke

If the front crawl is the get-there-quick stroke, the backstroke is the stop-and-smell-the-roses stroke. It's fun and relaxing, and breathing is easy. Because you don't have to concentrate much on breathing, it's easy to focus on the rest of the body. Although the body position is the same, the backstroke is actually easier to do than back floating, because the movement helps to keep the body in position.

The first stage

By this point, your child has the advantage of having learned to float on their back, to kick, and to streamline their body position. All of this is the foundation for starting to learn the backstroke.

Floating on their back has prepared your child to keep their body horizontal and their head in line with the rest of their body. This is the necessary starting point for the backstroke.

Step 1

To start to learn the backstroke, ask your child to put their arms in streamline position while they float on their back and kick. Have them practice this for a while to get a feel for moving while they're on their back.

Tip

Be sure to track their position in the pool for them and give them plenty of feedback about where they are in relation to the sides or end of the pool. Later they'll learn to do this himself.

Step 2

Have your child pull one of their arms from streamline position through the water to their thigh. Have them lift their arm to return it to streamline position and then try the same thing with their other arm. Have them practice alternating their arms this way until they feel comfortable with it.

Tip

As with the front crawl, have your child visualize reaching for something just beyond their grasp above their head and to look up. This will help to counteract the tendency to bend at the waist.

Step 3

At first, your child might have to concentrate so hard on moving their arms that they forget to keep kicking. Don't worry about this. After they've gotten some experience moving their arms, gently remind them to kick. Work on this until your child is comfortable stroking with their arms and kicking continuously.

The next stage

Step 1

As with the front crawl, ask your child to think about grabbing a handful of water and pulling it down to their hip. Have them imagine that they're trying to keep the water from falling out of their hand. They should keep their fingers together and their palm gently cupped. How does it feel?

Step 2

Have your child concentrate on pushing the water toward their feet, not pushing down on the water. As they become comfortable with the movement, have them imagine that they're trying to push the water in a straight line from their head to their feet. This will encourage them to bend their elbow instead of stroking through the water with a straight arm.

Bending their elbow will allow them to generate more power with less effort. It will also keep them from wasting energy moving their arm down through the water. As the arm approaches the end of the stroke near their thigh, they'll straighten it to get the most out of that pushing water toward their feet.

Step 3

Once they're comfortable with this, let them practice it until kicking simultaneously comes naturally.

Step 4

As with the front crawl, your child will naturally start to play with the timing of their arm movements. It's particularly easy to do when they're practicing the backstroke, because they don't have to worry about taking a breath.

Encourage them to experiment. What happens if you start moving one arm back while the other arm is pulling back? What happens if you start moving one arm back while the other arm is returning to streamline position? Foster an awareness of timing and the different results different approaches to timing yield.

For the best recovery to the streamline starting position, they'll bring their arm straight through the air.

And, finally

Step 1

Your child needs to learn to be aware of where they are in the pool and when they're approaching a wall. If you're practicing in a pool with lanes and flags, this is easier. Have them pay attention to the flags above their head and keep an arm outstretched once they pass them. How long does it take to reach the wall once they've seen the flags? How many strokes?

If there are no flags suspended above the pool you're using, help your child to pick out another landmark that they can spot from the corner of their eye or by slightly turning their head. Make sure to let them know that you won't let them bump their head into the wall while they're practicing.

Step 2

If you want to work on refining the backstroke, have your child focus on the position of their hand as it enters the water. Their palm should face away from their body, and their little finger should enter the water first.

Step 3

The rotation of their shoulders will create a twisting motion in their torso and a gentle rolling feeling. Have them notice this and the effect of their kicking on stabilizing themselves.

Step 4

The backstroke is a perfect stroke for paying attention to keeping the kick small, gentle, fluid, and from the hip. Point out how only their toes will break the surface of the water and their feet will create very little splash.

Turning their head to breathe

Your child doesn't need to learn to turn their head to breathe to be safe in the water, but if they want to do a true crawl or to swim as fast as possible, they'll want to.

At the end of the process, your child will learn that, as their body rolls so that they're mostly on their side, they'll turn their head just slightly so that it's out of the water and they can breathe in through their mouth. They'll time the breath so that they'll be looking through a triangle formed by the bent recovering arm and the surface of the water.

The first stage

Step 1

You can practice on dry land. Have your child put their hands on the edge of a table and move their feet until they can position their upper body into a streamline position on a plane with the surface of the table. Have them hold onto the edge of the table with one hand—let's call this the stroking arm—and gently touch the table with the other hand—let's call this the recovering arm. Ask them to twist their torso, turning so that the shoulder of the recovering arm lifts toward the ceiling. The hand of the recovering arm might lift a few inches off the table, too. Have them notice the position of their head relative to the recovering arm.

Step 2
Practice the same thing in the pool. Have your child stand in the shallow end and hold onto the edge of the pool with their upper body in streamline position. Ask them to put their face in the water and twist their torso. Does their mouth come just barely out of the water? Do they need to twist their head just a little more to get their mouth clear?

At this point, your child shouldn't be relying on turning their head to breathe. They can stand up straight whenever they want to take a breath. They should concentrate, though, on turning their head directly to the side instead of lifting it up.

Step 3
Practice the same exercise holding onto the edge of the pool with the whole body in streamline position, gently kicking instead of standing. Once your child is comfortable with this, have them try to take a breath during one of their turns. Don't try to move into this too quickly, and don't try to establish a rhythm right away.

Step 4
After they're comfortable with taking one breath, have them try to establish a rhythm. Turn, turn and breathe, turn, turn and breathe. Make sure they understand that they don't have to breathe every time they turn. When they practice, have them breathe on the same side every time.

Step 5
Next have your child practice expelling air while their head is underwater so that they're ready to inhale as soon as their head is above the water. If they've already learned to blow bubbles, they know how to expel air while their head is under water. Ask them to expel all the air then twist their head and body to inhale.

The next stage
Now that your child has extensive practice breathing by turning their head, it's time to combine it with the front crawl.

Step 1

Have them swim from one side of the pool to the other in the shallow end, so that they're confident that they can just put their feet down to stand anytime they want. Walk next to them while they swim to provide them with an extra sense of security.

Step 2

Once they're swimming, the skill can be broken into two parts: the torso rotation and the head rotation and breathing. Start by working on torso rotation. Have your child do a couple of strokes of front crawl.

When they would normally pop up to take a breath, have them roll onto their back and do a few strokes of the backstroke instead. The point of this exercise is to help them get a feel for keeping their body horizontal throughout the rotation.

Tip

If they have a tendency to lift their head, they'll feel how it tips their body out of position. A simple verbal reminder like "turn don't lift" or "turn don't tilt" should help them to focus on keeping their head in line with their body. If verbal reminders not to lift their head aren't enough to help them with the movement, you can have them practice rolling from a streamline position into a back float position while you support them.

Step 3

Once they're comfortable rotating their torso all the way over, have them practice doing the front crawl, rotating their torso and turning their head, but not taking a breath.

Step 4

Once they've done that a few times, they're ready to combine the skills: turn their torso and head during the stroke and take a breath through the space between the recovery arm and the water.

Have them swim from one side of the pool to the other, practicing turning their head to breathe just once each lap and using popup breathing the rest of the time.

Tip
Back on land, you can reinforce the idea of turning-not-lifting their head by having them lie on their back on the ground and turn their head directly side to side.

And, finally

Step 1
After your child has gotten the hang of turning their head for single breaths, you can increase it to a sequence of them, starting with two and working their way to the width and then the length of the pool using this kind of breathing.

Keep in mind that they won't need a breath every stroke. Typically, a pattern of taking a breath every other or every third stroke on one side is comfortable.

Tip
It's likely that they'll swallow some water and some air during this process. Warn them in advance that water might get in their mouth and practice having them spit it out. Make sure to give them plenty of opportunities to burp so that they'll avoid getting a stomachache from swallowing air.

And all the steps beyond
When they're comfortable with the process of turning their head to breathe, you can help them refine their form.

- Have them think of pointing their nose toward the bottom of the pool when they're not taking a breath.

- Have them focus on having their head turned just enough, so that their mouth is clear of the water but the water is still touching the outer edge of their eye.

- Have them focus on swiveling their head instead of lifting it.

Internalizing the skills

Some of these skills will come easily to your child. Some might be tougher to get. With your help and plenty of practice, your child will have a great time learning to swim.

By the time they start practicing the front crawl, blowing bubbles and kicking will be second nature. With enough practice the front crawl will be second nature, too. Have fun with it! These weeks or months will fly by, but they'll pay off for the rest of your child's life.

Chapter 11
Life: A Game, a Play, a Bowl of Cherries

Playing is a safe way for the brain to learn, because you can use your imagination without risk. You can create elaborate risky situations and practice problem-solving techniques to get out of them, all in your head without any real-life risk. Playing is a major way that kids learn new things. Take advantage of this when you're trying to help your child learn to swim.

Some animals play only when they're maturing and stop when they're adults. Humans' ability to play through adulthood makes us flexible and good at learning new things. (Turns out dogs are another species that continue to play throughout their lives. That's why you can indeed teach an old dog new tricks.) Play improves our ability to learn and remember.

What makes things fun? Different people enjoy different forms of play. Some people look for pleasure, whether it's physical, mental or emotional. Some people look for wonder, excitement, and anticipation. Some people look for surprise and the unexpected. Some people look for the feelings they get when they use their bodies.

Knowing your child and the kinds of play they like, you can create games that will captivate and motivate them.

How does your child have fun? Are they mentally oriented? Do they joke around, with silliness, cleverness, practical jokes, and slapstick? Do they love using their imagination, either creating or enjoying stories? Does your child build elaborate fantasy games, like playing spy or having tea parties? Does your child have favorite princesses or superheroes from movies? Incorporate their favorite characters from books and movies in games.

Do they like making a plan and seeing it come together? Does your child like making things or doing projects? Do they enjoy learning new ideas? Are they competitive? Do they like winning and keeping score?

Are they more physically oriented? Do they enjoy exploring new places or sensations? Do they like collecting things? Do they love to use their body, feeling the thrill of the wind rushing through their hair as they race on their bike?

You can use what you know about your child to design the games and activities that will appeal to them most. The secret side benefits of playing with your child: not only are you building your relationship but you're also strengthening both of your brains.

Here's a list of more than 150 games and activities that will help get you started:

Getting into the pool

1. How would different animals get into the pool? Try it like a cat, a bear, a butterfly, and a hummingbird. How about a crocodile—check out some cool YouTube footage of that—a duck, a frog, a tiger, a dog, or a hippo?

2. Have your child pretend they're scooting off the end of a slide.

3. Have them pretend they're a plant pushing its roots down into the ground.

4. Have them pretend they're a boat going down a ramp into the water.

5. If they're ready to practice jumping in, have them jump in holding their body like an arrow, like a pencil, and—stand back for the classic—like a cannonball.

6. Ask them if they can slip into the water without moving it at all.

7. Place objects at the bottom of the pool marking the distance from the wall at 6", a foot, 18", and so on. Have you child try to reach to you when you stand at the 6" line. Take a step back and try at the one-foot line. See how far they can go. At some point, they'll have to start jumping.

8. Ask them how quickly they can get from the edge of the pool into the pool, making sure that they're still being safe. Count off the seconds. This is particularly good for kids who have to work up their nerve to get in.

9. Have them scoot into the pool from sitting on their bottom. Next, have them lie on their tummy and scoot back feet-first into the pool. Have them compare the two techniques. Which do they like better?

10. Have your child imagine they're getting into a big bowl of pudding. How about a pool full of milk? Jell-o? What else could the water be that would be fun to get into? Whipped cream? Mud?

11. Use "one for the money, two for the show, three to get ready, and four to go" to help them prepare themselves for the "go" moment of getting into the pool.

12. Make funny noises when they get in. Kerplop!

Feeling the water

13. How does the water feel? Does it feel…prickly? No! Slippery? Bubbly? Sparkly? Bumpy? Smooth? Silky? Soft? Rough? Sloshy? Rubbery?

14. Does the water feel like pudding? Baby food? Milk? Juice? Watermelon? (Throw in some choices that are really silly.)

15. What does being in the water feel like? Does it feel like flying? Like being an astronaut? Like going down a slide? Like jumping in a bouncy house? Like swinging on a swing? Like riding a bike?

16. How would a mermaid move? A fish? A dolphin? A whale? A shark? A sea star? A crab? A pirate? A penguin? A seagull? An octopus?

17. Use a foam noodle to tow your child around the pool.

18. Paint each other's faces with the water.

19. Bounce up and down. How high can you go? How low?

20. Swish through the water and stop abruptly.

21. Play rock-a-bye baby.

22. Have your child hold your hands while you walk backwards. Zigzag through the water.

23. Hold very still. Do you still feel the water on your skin?

24. Make the biggest, loudest splash possible.

Holding onto the wall and climbing out

25. Be like a monkey. Be like a crab. Be like a spider, an octopus, a sea star, a lemur. Be like a ladybug holding onto a blade of grass. How would all of these animals move along the wall?

26. Have your child move their hands like cars in a traffic jam. One car has to move before the other can move into position next to it. No passing!

27. Have your child pretend to be a rock climber or a mountain climber. How about a knight or a princess climbing up or down a tower? How about an acrobat?

28. Have your child experiment with using their feet to walk along the wall and help their hands. Can they lift them up so they're close to their hands? Can they stretch them down so they're flat against the wall and only their toes are helping?

29. Alternate hands with your child. Stand behind them and put your hand next to theirs. When they moves their hand, move yours next to theirs or leapfrog over it. Keep them guessing about which you'll do.

30. Have your child see how far they can move along the wall. Can they go all the way around the pool?

31. Draw a finish line on the edge of the pool with chalk. Which hand gets there first?

32. Time them. Can they get faster?

33. Can they go hand over hand like they're turning a steering wheel?

34. Make up a super hero story with your child as the star. "The super duper swimmer went hand-to-hand along the edge of the pool...." What happens next?

35. Can your child hang on with just their fingertips on the edge and their head low to the water? Can the people outside the pool even see them when they try it this way? Very sneaky.

36. Can they do pushups, pushing away and pulling back with their arms (without letting go of the wall)?

Blowing bubbles

37. On land, practice blowing raspberries on each other's tummies.

38. Have your child blow through a straw into a glass of soapy water and see what happens. Why doesn't that happen in the pool?

39. Have your child make their bubble blowing sound like a boat. How about a helicopter? How about a fart? (Kids love fart jokes. What are you gonna do.)

40. Play this game:

    While your child blows bubbles, you sing: "Bubbles, bubbles, bubbles..."
    Have them lift their head and clap. Do this three times.
    The fourth time, you sing: "Bubbles, bubbles..."
    And they lift their head and slap the water while you both yell, "POP!"

41. Have your child pretend to be a little fish blowing tiny bubbles in the water. Now have tehm be a big fish blowing big bubbles. Real fish have actually been observed playing bubble games. Fish like to play!

42. Time them. How long can they blow bubbles without stopping?

43. What happens if you try to blow bubbles while you're laughing? Have them try it. Tell them some jokes. Can they still blow bubbles?

44. Have your child try to take a breath so big that it stretches their whole face. Have them look at it in the mirror. Does it make them laugh? Can they let the air out very slowly? Very fast? Very loudly? How long can they hold the breath?

45. Have your child try to blow just one bubble at a time.

46. Have your child pretend they're playing a musical instrument. Which instrument are they playing? A saxophone? A bagpipe? Have them use their hands, too. You make the instrument's noise for them. (It's even better if you're no good at it.)

47. Have your child pretend they're a hamster filling its cheek pouches with air. (Hamsters really do this when they're getting ready to go for a swim.)

Putting their head underwater

48. Play scuba diver. Have your child duck under and look around while you swim past them like a fish.

49. Play duck. Quack on the surface together and then dunk your heads under to look for food. Did you find any?

50. Have your child put their head underwater while you say something above the water. Can they figure out what you said? How about if you say it while you're both underwater?

51. Play lost city of Atlantis. Let me know if you find it.

52. Have your child move their head around underwater to see how it feels. What happens to their hair? Does it swish around? Is it

long enough for them to see it? Go under with them and let them watch and feel your hair (if you have any).

53. Have your child put their head underwater and lift up very slowly, until their eyes are just above the water. Have them pretend they're a crocodile looking for prey, and you're the prey. Let them pounce!

54. Make a series of cards with words or pictures on them so that viewed in sequence they tell a story. Put each card in a waterproof plastic bag and show your child one card at a time each time they put their head under. The suspense!

55. Have your child see how long they can stay underwater. Go under together and hold up one finger for each second you stay under, starting with staying under for just one second before surfacing and working your way up to staying under for ten seconds. (Let your child guide you. Don't push them to hold their breath longer than is comfortable for them.)

56. Have your child jump from the side into the pool so that they go under for a second before you scoop them into your arms and bring them to the surface.

57. Play astronaut. Does it feel weightless under there?

58. Is it hard to stay under? Have your child put their head under and pop up as fast, high, and hard as they can.

59. Have your child jump up and down in the shallow end. Have them squat down and push up to see how high they can jump. Can they be as springy as a kangaroo?

60. Play Ring around the Rosie with them. Go underwater when you all fall down.

61. Hold them on your back and jump up and down together, going under every time you land or every few jumps. Make sure they're prepared for it when you go underwater.

Kicking

62. Have your child kick while you tow them. Let them determine how fast you go based on how fast they kick.

63. Have them pretend to be a duck. Flip those flippers!

64. Have your child sit in a chair and see how fast they can kick. How slow. How straight they can keep their legs. Now try it in the water.

65. Have your child make the same kicking motion with their arms. How does it feel? Is it the same? What are the differences?

66. Have your child sit in a chair and alternate pointing and flexing their feet. Are they fast enough to keep you from pinching their toes when they point them?

67. Have your child kick like different animals: a kangaroo, a donkey, a goat, a rabbit, a frog. What are other kicking animals? Is there any animal that kicks like a person swimming?

68. Have your child be a soccer player trying to kick a ball down the field, keeping it under control all the time. Use your hand as the ball.

69. Use a drum or make one out of a cardboard cylinder and enough masking tape to cover the opening entirely. Have your child sit in a chair and kick the drum with their flutter-kicking feet. What kind of music can they make? Can they make rhythms? Can they kick very steadily and quickly?

70. Have your child imagine that there's a giant rubber band around their ankles and that they're stretching it with every kick.

Gliding in streamline or torpedo position

71. Place clues around the edge of the swimming pool. Point your child to the first clue and have them glide to it. The first clue leads to the next, and so on. The last stop should have a treat: a joke, a medal, or another prize your child will like.

72. Race! Have your child glide while you walk through the water. Who can make it to the other side first?

73. Play catch with your gliding child as the ball. (You'll need another grownup for this one.)

74. Have your child pretend to be a surfboard. How about a sailboat? A kayak?

75. Have your child pretend to be a dolphin. A slippery seal. An otter. A fish.

76. Have your child pretend to be an arrow or a spear that you throw across the surface of the water.

77. Have them push off from the side and glide toward you. Can they get you?

78. Have them pretend to be a rocket. An airplane.

79. Have them pretend to be Superman flying through the water. (Both arms forward please. I'm not sure Superman understood aerodynamics thoroughly.)

80. How far can your child glide before they have to stand up?

81. What happens if they push off from the side but don't kick? How about if they push off and do their best kicking?

82. Put interesting objects on the bottom of the pool along the path they'll follow. Can they figure out what they are? Can you surprise them with anything?

Popup breathing

83. How high can your child push themselves by pushing down into the water with their arms?

84. Sing "Pop Goes the Weasel" and have them pop up on the word "Pop."

85. Have them pretend to be a sea turtle popping their head up for a breath.

86. Have them play with pushing their arms *up* to see how far *down* they'll go.

87. Have them imagine that they're a prairie dog popping its head out of its hole. How about a meerkat?

88. Have them practice on the ground, lying on their stomach and pressing their arms down while they lift their head.

89. Have them pretend they're a front loader lifting its bucket to get a load of air.

90. How many times can they take a popup breath before they have to put their feet down? Can they make it all the way across the pool?

Body shape and position

91. At a playground, have your child hang from the bars or rings. Does their body feel long? Does it feel loooong? Have them

stand on the ground reaching for a bar or ring that's too high. How does it feel?

92. At home, have them watch themselves in the mirror, standing with their arms above their head. Hold something just above their fingertips and have them stretch to reach it. How does it feel?

93. Have them glide through the water like different animals: a fish, a dolphin, an otter, a seal. How would a pig go through water? Is that a helpful position?

94. Have them try different shapes. Absolutely straight. With a curved back like a ship's hull. Back slightly rounded like the bottom of a surfboard.

95. Can they do a somersault in the water? How about a backwards somersault.

96. What happens if they spread their limbs out like a sea star and then quickly pull them in to their sides so that they're as straight as an eel?

Treading water

97. Have them move in the water like a duck. Like a dog. Like a bear. Like an elephant. Show them videos of land animals in the water. What's as fun as watching an elephant swim?

98. How long can they stop moving before they start to sink?

99. Play catch while you're both treading water.

100. Point out interesting clouds or planes overhead to encourage them to keep their head up. Is that a hot air balloon festival? Amazing!

101. Have them pretend they're playing different sports in the water and see how it works. What if they swing an imaginary baseball bat and runs? How about if they pretend to paddle a canoe? How about boxing or kung fu? Swinging an imaginary golf club? Playing imaginary wall ball? Doing ballet? How about hip-hop?

102. Pretend you're on a sightseeing bus together. What do you spot going by? What do they spot? Can you make it as imaginative as *And to Think That I saw It on Mulberry Street*, by Dr. Seuss?

103. Have your child pretend that treading water is a dance. How graceful can they make it?

104. Sing songs. Can they stay afloat during the claps in B-I-N-G-O?

105. Have them pretend they're riding a unicycle across a tightrope. How about biking through the mountains? You provide the commentary.

106. Have them pretend they're digging down through the water to the other side of the earth. How's their progress? What sights do you see?

107. Draw an imaginary circle around them and see if they can stay inside it.

108. Pretend they're a marionette and you're pulling strings that move their arms and legs.

109. Time them. How long can they keep it up?

110. Have them pretend they're trying to make whipped cream out of the water with their legs. How's it coming?

Moving underwater

111. Put coins or sinking toys on the bottom of the pool for your child to pick up.

112. Make a path of objects in the bottom of the pool and have them follow it, touching each one as they go.

113. Play astronaut. Play deep-sea diver.

114. Play "head, shoulders, knees, and toes." Head and shoulders can be above the surface.

115. Be a hippo. Did you know that hippos can't swim? They walk on the surface underwater.

116. Play Marco Polo.

117. Have them pretend to be an undercover agent trying to get from place to place as quietly as possible.

118. Have them try to sneak up on you.

119. Have them pretend to be animals: a fish, a whale, a dinosaur, an otter, a seal, a frog, an octopus.

120. Have them hold onto the pool wall and climb down the wall until they touch the bottom.

121. Can they sit on the bottom? Is it easy or hard?

122. Teach them some synchronized swimming moves. Can they touch the bottom with their hands and stick their legs straight up out of the water? Point those toes!

123. Have them pretend they're a submarine exploring the ocean floor.

124. Can they grab your toes?

Back float

125. How flat can your child make their body? Can they balance something on their belly?

126. What do they see above them? What do they hear if they close their eyes?

127. Otters lie on their backs and put their food on their bellies to clean it. Have your child be an otter cleaning its food.

128. Have them bend at the waist to grab their toes. How fast do they sink?

129. Put a hand beneath their head and gently move them around the pool as they float.

130. Make gentle waves near them by moving your body up and down. Does that change the way floating feels? How about if you make the water really rough?

131. Pretend you're a magician and they're you're assistant. You're making them levitate.

132. Have them pretend they're lying in bed. Is this softer than their bed?

133. Sing songs about boats and water:

    Row, Row, Row Your Boat
    Michael, Row Your Boat Ashore
    A Sailor Went to Sea
    Anchors Aweigh
    My Bonnie Lies over the Ocean
    Take Me to the River (if that's your jam)

134. What happens if they kick gently while they float? What if they kick harder? What if they flick their feet? How about if they keep their toes pointed? Flexed?

135. Have your child pretend to be Snow White or Sleeping Beauty.

136. Have them pretend to be a piece of driftwood. A leaf on the water. A lily pad.

Front crawl

137. Place clues around the edge of the swimming pool the same way you did in #71.

138. Toss a floating ball or Frisbee and have your child swim to it. Have them tread water while they toss it back to you.

139. Race against each other.

140. Race with imagination. What's the rush? They're Paul Revere riding to alert colonists that the British are coming. They've got to get to home base before they're thrown out.

141. Have them pretend their arms are a windmill. A pinwheel. A fan.

142. Play tag. Can they catch you?

143. Pretend they're a cab driver taking you to different spots around the pool. Swim next to them to get there.

144. Have them pretend to be an Olympic swimmer.

145. Have them pretend to be a racecar. A sailboat. A kayak.

146. Pretend they're swimming in the ocean. In a mountain lake. In a fast-moving river. In a lazy stream. What sights do they see? What adventures do they have?

147. What animal is the best swimmer? Have them be that animal. What animal is the most awkward swimmer? Have them be that animal.

148. Play Marco Polo. (See #116.)

149. Have them count how many handfuls of water they've pushed to their feet. How many got away?

Backstroke

150. Tickle their toes when they break the surface.

151. Loosely tie a string to their toe. Hold onto the other end and have them pretend to tow you. (Careful! This is just pretend.)

152. Have them try to swim in the straightest line they can. Pick a spot on the opposite side of the pool and mark it with chalk. Go! How close did they get?

153. Have them guess when their hand will touch the wall.

154. Have them follow you just by the sound of your voice.

155. Can they sing and swim at the same time?

156. Make everything backwards while they're doing the backstroke. Can they talk backwards? Can you tell each other stories from end to beginning? When you get out of the pool, put on your clothes backwards. Try explaining that to the rest of the family when you get home. They probably won't understand you if you're talking backwards.

157. Can they crisscross the pool until they've covered every square foot of it? What parts of the pool have they not visited yet?

158. Have them call out whenever they spot something in the sky, even if it's just the flags over the pool of a tree branch.

159. Tell them their favorite family stories or fairy tales while they swim.

160. Put a lightweight toy on their belly and see if they can swim without letting it fall.

161. Are there any other activities you would do moving headfirst on your back? Would they be safe? How about sledding? Talk about the gory possibilities.

Turning their head to breathe

162. Have them pretend to be a log rolling in the water from stomach to back to stomach again. (I know, I know, logs don't have stomachs.) Have them do it themselves. Now you roll them.

163. Can they roll in the water like an otter? Go to an aquarium or watch videos of otters playing.

164. Have them sit in a chair with you kneeling by their side. Hold an object in your hand. Have them follow it with just their eyes as you start to move it behind them. At some point, they'll need to turn their head to see it. Laugh and cheer when they do. Make sure you move it so that they don't have to lift their head to see it.

165. Have them pretend they have to look beside them to see if there's another swimmer there. Sometimes there will be: you making funny faces.

166. Every time they turn their head to take a breath, hold an interesting object in the best spot for them to see it when their head is in the right position.

167. Can they pretend they're an owl turning its head?

Made in the USA
San Bernardino, CA
25 June 2017